YOUR BRAND SUCKS
How to ignite a brand that doesn't.

Text Copyright 2020 -Ernie Harker
Cover Art and Illustrations- Ernie Harker

Table of Contents

	Foreword	*v*
	Acknowledgements	*vii*
	Introduction	*viii*
PART I	**UNDERSTAND BRANDING**	**1**
	Branding Crash Course	3
	Branding Begins with Personality	3
	But where to start?	5
	Is Branding Just a Bunch of Fluff?	7
	Why You Should Care About Branding	8
	Assemble Your Brand Trust	11
PART II	**FIRE UP YOUR BRAND STRATEGY!**	**13**
	F – Find Your 'Brand Spark'	15
	I – Identify Your Target Customer	32
	R – Realize Your Core Belief	40
	E – Establish Your Brand Adjectives	47
	Review and Test	57
PART III	**THE BUILDING BLOCKS OF YOUR BRAND**	**63**
	Establish Your Brand's Look and Feel	65
	Imagery & Pictures	70
	Patterns, Textures, and Materials	75
	Typography	78
	Vocabulary	80

PART IV	ASSEMBLING THE PARTS	89
	Design Your Logo	93
	Develop a Snappy Tagline	96
	Develop a Brand Bible (aka Brand Design Style Guide)	100
PART V	PUTTING YOUR BRAND TO WORK	107
	Print and Digital Graphic Design	109
	Wear Your Brand	114
	Developing Names for Titles, Products, Services, and Companies	120
	Branded Ads	135
	Charities and Sponsorships	140
	Three, two, one, liftoff!	142

Afterword   144

About the Author   145

Foreword

When any of us pick up a book, we all hope it will deliver on its promises, whether it is a book of poems, short stories, a novel or, as is the case here, a book filled with useful and invaluable information - a book that informs and educates. We want it to be a book that makes us feel glad we read it when we get to the end.

From the book's title *Your Brand Sucks,* you should be able to sense that it doesn't mess around. You will quickly discover it is plain talking; it tells you exactly how it is and talks to you in a language you will understand. It is not full of advertising jargon that only 'creatives' will 'get'.

You can also feel confident that all the information in the book has value, because the author backs up what he tells you with real-life examples of companies he has worked with, and these are companies whose names you will know and recognize. The author doesn't just tell you what will work, he'll actually prove it does!

If you are involved in advertising and branding, there will be some familiar territory in here, but there's a big chance you will also discover and learn something new that will help you add to your arsenal of productive knowledge.

If you are a business owner with an established product or brand, this is the proverbial "must read." Why? Because you will either discover your existing brand is on point, or *Your Brand Sucks* will not only tell you why it sucks, it will tell you how to fix it and give you the confidence to go ahead with a rebrand, especially if that is what is already at the back of your mind.

If you have a product or service you are just about to take to market, then you have found your branding bible. When it comes to creating your brand, not only will you discover what to do and why, this book also tells you what not to do, and why.

There is a saying: "Those who can, do, those who can't, teach." There should be an addition to that saying though: "Those who can do both are very few and far between." The author, Ernie Harker, is one of those very few.

- David Dundas

Acknowledgements

Considering my ADHD brain, finishing this book would have been impossible for me without help. First and foremost, I want to recognize my wife Wendy, who allowed me to pour hundreds of hours into writing and editing this book instead of insisting I clean the dishes or watch Downton Abbey with her. I want to ask my kids to forgive me for ignoring them while engrossed in this enterprise. I also want to thank my good friend and former boss Aaron Simpson, who at a critical crossroads, encouraged me with the words, "There may be lots of books about branding, but none by you told in your voice." I also want to express my appreciation to my editors Emily Price and David Dundas, who helped me organize my thoughts and wordsmith my prose to be more palatable than a 3rd-grade book report.

I also wish to express my sincere gratitude to the friends and family who agreed to review portions of this book and provide their helpful feedback.

Introduction

Are your competitors getting all of the attention with their attractive imagery, clever phrasing, engaging stories, and amazing culture? Are you frustrated or worried that a competitor with an inferior product is eating away at your business?

Great brands are easy to identify. People are drawn to them, like gravity, and are loyal to them because brand directors intentionally design them to elicit specific thoughts, feelings, and attitudes. I've helped many companies develop brands and know from experience that great branding is not the product of big budgets, it's the product of a deliberate strategy and consistent execution. Both are within reach of companies of all sizes.

In this book, I'll explain why most companies develop a brand with a look and feel that doesn't fit, and never did, right from the start. They struggle for years to make it work. Other companies evolve and outgrow their original, effective brands and battle to re-assert their relevance through ineffective, often detrimental rebranding.

For more than two decades I've helped many companies develop meaningful brands and I've learned what works and what doesn't. I've discovered that the best process for brand discovery and development is the same, regardless of which industry you're in, which will be revealed to you in full as you read through this book.

Because you're reading this book, chances are you already have an amazing product or service or have one in mind that is destined to add great value to the world. Your business deserves a look and feel that grabs your customers' attention and tells them, in an instant, what it's all about. Additionally, because your customers are not always immediately in the market to buy your product or service, you'll need to create something so memorable and remarkable that your business will be the first they recall when the time is right.

Whether you're a seasoned company that needs a brand course correction, or a small business startup that needs to establish a brand, this book is for you. It will reveal the most efficient, comprehensive, and effective approach you can adopt to establish a solid brand foundation and create the most fitting visual and verbal language to express it. Through the book's chapters, I'll guide you through the universal building blocks of effective brand development and take you, step by step, through a proven, successful, and effective process to create a brand that is authentic to your organization and, more important, is remarkable to your customers.

So, why should you listen to me? After all, my name is Ernie, and everybody knows that's a nerd's name. In fact, it might be helpful to think of me as a branding nerd. After all, I've spent over twenty-four years in the advertising and marketing industry as an illustrator, animator, writer, producer, designer, creative director, and brand strategist. I'm also the owner of a small business and an avid entrepreneur. I've worked with auto dealerships, residential developers, fitness equipment manufacturers, storage companies, dentists, ad agencies, and tech companies. I have worked with Chuck Norris on his bottled water brand and even had the 'pleasure' of being put in a chokehold by him! One of my greatest success stories was converting a cowboy-western-themed convenience store into a three-billion-dollar outdoor, adventure-themed brand.

I give presentations on brand development to organizations across the country. Branding is my superpower.

I also know what it's like to wear many hats as an entrepreneur and work with a shoestring budget. I've produced a TV travel series, an animated video series, written and illustrated a children's book, authored a how-to-draw book, and even started a YouTube channel.

I want to share this background with you to help you understand that I've likely stood in shoes similar to yours, whether you're a senior-level executive or the owner of a small business, and I know that what I can share with you will help you build a successful brand.

The Problem

For too many decades, brands have been built the wrong way!

I confess I wasn't very good at building brands at first because I followed the same 'shoot-a-moving-target' process that everybody else in the design industry used.

Here is a typical scenario: A client would hire my company to design a corporate identity package (logo, letterhead, and business card). The client would have a vague idea of what they wanted and would explain: "I'll know it when I see it." The task for us designers was to create something that hit a bullseye without being certain where the target was located.

We would begin with some competitive research to make sure our ideas weren't similar to other brands. We would use a shotgun approach by designing dozens of rough concepts and seeing which ones hit the target, judged by the client's personal preferences. As often as not, more targets would emerge as various people, both within and outside the company, vocalized their thoughts and feelings, each offering their opinion based on their own personal experiences and biases.

It often went like this:

HR Director: "I don't like red. It feels angry to me. We're not an angry company!"

CEO: "I like red because it's bold and gets attention. That's why stop signs are red!"

CFO: "I'm just not feeling it. I'm sure I'll know it when I see it."

Marketing Director: "What if we went with purple? Our competitors don't use purple in their brand, so we'll stand out for sure!"

Director of Technology: "I showed it to my niece who is studying design at university and she doesn't like it."

It was like herding cats! The team didn't have a shared vision of the personality of the brand which would serve as their foundation stone on which to build creative decisions. They also hadn't identified the emotions they wanted their customers to experience with the brand. Because they weren't trained to understand how colors, fonts, shapes and composition conveyed specific personality and elicited specific emotional reactions, they wielded their opinions like children wielding scalpels.

To help expedite the brand development process, save clients time and money, and to save my own sanity, I engineered a brand development process that prevented my clients from constantly moving the target based on their personal interpretations or emotional states. Instead, I would guide my clients through the development of a **brand strategy** for creative decisions, such as the design for logos and other marketing and advertising materials. The process proved to offer much more than a stable platform for developing a brand, it crystallized company vision, purpose and personality. It gave everyone a compass to ensure they were all moving, cohesively, in the same direction.

Breaking Down the Book

In Part I, you'll learn the basics of branding and some common mistakes to avoid. It will be a crash course in **brand development** that will open your eyes and mind.

In Part II, you will be guided through the four steps of FIRE-ing up your **brand strategy**. Each step asks you to make an important decision on a specific position that will define your brand and influence everything you do thereafter.

F- You will be asked to **Find Your Brand Spark**- the meaningful attributes that make your company unique and help your business stand out from the competition.

I- You will be asked to **Identify Your Target Customer**—that segment of the population most likely to recognize and pay for your special difference, so that you don't waste time and money on those who aren't so likely.

R- You will be asked to **Realize Your Core Belief**- Here, I'll guide you through the process of discovering the conviction that drives your company and how you can use it to create zealous followers.

E- You will be asked to **Establish Your Brand Adjectives**– I'll show you how to select a set of adjectives that describe your brand that can't be attributed to any other business in your industry. They will influence the design, colors, textures, images, fonts, vocabulary, tone, voice, sound, and personality of your brand in the expression of website, apps, products, packaging, advertising, and videos, etc.

When these questions have been answered and the key leaders of your company are in agreement, the decisions are documented in the form of a **brand strategy**. I've created a free workbook you can use to record your answers, so make sure you download the *Ignite Your Brand* workbook from https://ernburn.com/kindling.

Once you've completed the four FIRE steps, you'll then be guided through the process of stress testing your **brand strategy** to make sure it's on the right track.

In Part III, you will use your **brand strategy** as the background and rationale to design your **brand blueprints** in the form of colors, patterns, textures, fonts, image, vocabulary, and sound. These are the ingredients in your branding recipe that you'll use to create all of your advertising and marketing materials.

I'll also share numerous secrets and strategies to help you design a logo that will perfectly encapsulate the brand adjectives you chose in the fourth FIRE step E- Establish Your Brand Adjectives. You'll also learn how to write a snappy tagline, create a comprehensive **Brand Bible**, and learn how to use it to maintain brand consistency, ensuring that your amazing new brand will grow stronger and increase its focus with every decision you make.

In Part IV you'll put your **brand blueprints** to work, guiding the production of all of your sales and marketing tools like websites, brochures, packaging, interior and exterior design, uniforms, dress codes, charities, product names, and more.

My intention with this book is to provide you with an effective tool to help you create a powerful, memorable, and highly effective brand that will stand the test of time.

This book will detail a simple and effective, proven process you can follow to make sure your brand doesn't suck! It will ignite your brand by helping you develop a solid foundation for your company's personality and guide you through the selection of the verbal and visual language needed to help bring everything to life. You'll create a brand that your customers will love, and your competitors will envy.

Along the way, I'll occasionally invite you to "*Take Action.*" Here I want you to take a few minutes to perform requested "*Take

Action" exercises that will involve putting into practice what you have just learned about meaningful brand advancements.

However, before we launch your brand into orbit, you'll need to know about the catastrophic failures that most businesses experience on the launch pad so you can be sure to avoid them.

PART I
Understand Branding

Beware of false knowledge; it is more dangerous than ignorance.

– *George Bernard Shaw*

Branding Crash Course

I was asked to speak on the importance of branding at the 2017 marketing conference for a major fuel company where they were to unveil new branding for Phillips 66, Conoco, and 76.

I was on the edge of my seat among thousands of convenience store owners and franchise operators when the new street signs and interior and exterior design packages were unveiled.

I waited eagerly for a description of the unique personalities of each brand and how they were different to their fuel industry competitors. I waited to hear how each brand was going to make an emotional connection to its target customer. I waited to discover how the interior and exterior design packages would reinforce that unique personality.

I waited and waited.

Instead, they started talking about costs of construction.

I was like a six-year-old unwrapping a Christmas present only to discover a three-pack of underwear inside!

This experience demonstrated that even large, well-funded companies don't always understand that branding starts with an awareness of that company's personality and should not be approached exclusively as a graphic design problem.

Branding Begins with Personality

We all prefer to spend time with people based on their personalities. We are attracted to people based on their sense of humor, by how they talk, what they talk about, what they like to do, and how they react to situations. We identify them by how they look and what they wear.

The same is true for businesses. When products offer similar benefits, we prefer to do business with companies based on their personality, which is the expression of their brand.

Branding is the personality of your business. It's what influences all the decisions you make, from the products you develop to the language, look, and feel of your marketing materials. It is represented by ad campaigns, logos, packaging, interior and exterior design, digital media and what the company does and says in sponsorships, corporate affiliations, corporate slogans, terminology, corporate policy, community involvement, charitable giving, employee treatment, social media responses, and more. Branding is what creates an emotional relationship with your customers that gets them to pay top dollar for what you sell, and it's the emotional relationship that drives business.

The personality of your company is shaped by the values of the company leadership or founder and the role you believe your business plays in the world. This will be conveyed by the tone and language used in advertising, marketing, and on social media platforms. It will also be represented in merchandise, product packaging, social media, and other sales and marketing materials. Even the non-profit charities your company supports are a reflection of your company's personality. When you have a clear understanding of your company's personality, choosing the right graphic design elements to represent it and influence your customers is much easier to do.

Think about it—a construction company wouldn't dream of starting a project without a set of blueprints designed to meet the specific needs of the client, but when it comes to branding, most companies jump in swinging hammers. They approach branding as a graphic design exercise and start designing logos, choosing colors, and designing websites without first defining their **brand strategy**.

A **brand strategy** is a short document that explains exactly what makes your business different. It includes a detailed description of your ideal customer, what your company believes about your role in the industry, and a clear description of what you want those customers to feel and think about your business. It serves as a blueprint to ensure that the look and feel of the brand you are building will make your business profitable and easier to run. Skipping the development of a **brand strategy** results in a brand built on a shaky foundation that never quite fits the needs of the company and is destined for an expensive and painful rebuild when business doesn't do as well as expected.

But where to start?

In every organization there is usually someone responsible for embodying the brand. In small businesses it's almost always the entrepreneur or owner(s). These brand keepers intuitively know what the brand should say, how it should look, and how it should make people feel. They seem to be, or think they are, the only person with the insight to make decisions that strengthen the brand. They get frustrated when other leaders or employees don't see what is obvious to them. The cause of this frustration isn't the fault of smart, talented, and hard-working employees– it's often the result of the brand keepers not defining or sharing a **brand strategy**.

Imagine what kind of results your business could achieve if everyone who worked in and for your company had a clear vision of your **brand strategy.** This book will help you expedite the development of your **brand strategy** so you can build a brand worthy of a legacy.

When evaluating logos, graphic design, advertising messages, sponsorship opportunities, dress code, product development, or whatever, I often hear the question, "Which one do you like best?" That's a terrible question because it focuses on the personal preference of the person being asked. The question that should be asked is, "Which of these options is most in line with our **brand strategy**?" Without a **brand strategy**, everyone is making decisions based on their gut feelings.

The process of brand discovery exposes each company stakeholder's differences of strategy, opinion, and interpretation. This provides tremendous insight to see who is going to be a brand advocate and who will be a brand critic. Reaching an agreement on the four elements of **brand strategy** will require collaboration and discussion. Ultimately, it requires a high level of consensus because the decisions made in this process become the basis for designing the brand blueprints which describe how the brand should look and feel.

The **brand strategy** creates a lens for your brand that helps focus the right message in the right way to the right people. And, the point of it all is to make an emotional connection with your customers because when it comes to making purchase decisions, consumers aren't as pragmatic as they think they are.

This is why some people buy Subaru's and others buy Jeeps. Both of these brands offer vehicles that can transport you from point A to point B, but each brand has a different personality. One is aggressive and bold while the other is reserved and liberal. The brands we choose to buy or the brands we choose to purchase from reflect who we are or what we aspire to be. This is why creating a **brand strategy** and sticking to a **brand lens** is so crucial. Every use of the brand is another opportunity to reinforce the company's personality.

The strength and clarity of a brand comes from focusing all customer touch points through a singular **Brand Lens**. A **Brand Lens** is your brand ideal. It's how you want your business to look, feel, and be perceived. It is the heart of your brand and a construct that will help you stay focused on a singular vision or interpretation of your brand.

Is Branding Just a Bunch of Fluff?

I meet at least one individual in nearly every consulting opportunity that says something like, "Look, I hate to burst your bubble, but this whole effort is a waste of time. Branding is just a bunch of fluff. We should be spending our time on more important things."

I usually discover that these people consider themselves too smart for the "smoke and mirrors" of branding. They pride themselves on their intellect and think branding is a gimmick to cloud facts and dupe weak-minded people into buying inferior products.

It's true that great branding can effectively persuade consumers to buy inferior products, but why not use it to sell yours? It's a fiscal responsibility of the business to present its products or services in the best possible light.

I also point out that in order for their product or service to be considered by a potential customer, the company must first make an impression. It needs to get its customers' attention. Too many businesses play it safe. I remember consulting with a convenience store chain that asked me to help it refresh its brand to boost its business. Unfortunately, everyone kept shooting down ideas that were too bold. They didn't want to be embarrassed by standing out too much. WHAT!?! As far as I know, they are still doing what they've always done and risk facing a competitor with a brand people will talk about.

Branding isn't about duping people; it's about attracting attention and building a relationship. It's about consistently creating memorable and remarkable impressions over time to build trust and to persuade your prospect to prefer your product or service.

Businesses spend a considerable amount of time and money to get the attention of potential customers through advertising and marketing. Great branding isn't about spending more money; it's about making sure the money being spent is done so in the most effective way possible.

Why You Should Care About Branding

We like to think we're logical people making practical decisions based on hard data. We tend to think that people who make emotion-based decisions are weak minded and easily duped. However, when it comes to making purchase decisions, consumers aren't as pragmatic as we think they are. Business and brain-science research shows that how we feel strongly influences what we do, especially when it comes to our purchasing decisions. Branding is the art and science of creating an emotional connection that's easy to trigger.

Based on the messages we see in advertising, we would think people who wear Nike sneakers are empowered with world-class athleticism, guys who drink Bud Light have supermodel girlfriends and are fun to hang out with, and people who use Apple products are creative trendsetters. We know those ideas aren't actually true, but those marketing messages work because they appeal to our emotions.

According to Harvard Business Professor Gerald Zaltman, 95% of purchasing decisions are subconscious:

"Emotion is what really drives the purchasing behaviors, and also decision making in general. This idea is of great importance because it helps us realize that human beings are not as logical as we might imagine. And understanding this has significant implications for marketing, sales, and branding.

"For example, by only marketing the attributes of your product, you will likely generate lackluster results. And the poor results you receive are due to the fact you are completely missing the subconscious, human element in the decision-making process.

"Humans are driven by feelings. So, if you want the consumer to remember your product or brand, they must be engaged and impassioned by the interaction with your company."[1]

Antonio Damasio, a Professor of Neuroscience at University of Southern California, points to functional magnetic resonance imaging (fMRI) studies that show that when evaluating brands, consumers primarily use emotions (personal feelings and experiences) rather than information (brand attributes, features, and facts). His research also reveals that the consumer's emotional response to an ad has a far greater influence on their reported intent to buy a product than does the ad's content– by a factor of 3:1 for television commercials and 2:1 for print ads.[2]

When our physical need for food, water, and shelter have been satisfied, we crave significance, acceptance, love, and self-improvement. Successful companies use branding to connect their products or services to those emotional needs.

---

[1] Logan Chierotti, "Harvard Professor Says 95% of Purchasing Decisions Are Subconscious," Inc. Magazine, Mar 26, 2018

[2] Peter Noel Murray Ph.D., "How Emotions Influence What We Buy" Psychology Today- Feb 26, 2013

The product differences between brands are relatively small, such as Budweiser or Coors, Nike or Adidas, but there is a big difference in how those companies make you feel and think about them. Nike uses verbal and visual language such as images of high-performance athletes, taglines, sponsorships etc., which helps its audience feel empowered, fit, and successful. Bud Light carefully orchestrates its messages of cute girls being attracted to average-looking guys to suggest that drinking Bud Light will make you fun and attractive. As another example, Apple uses verbal language like "Think Different" and the visual language of beautifully designed products. This is done to suggest that if you're not using Apple products you're a mindless follower of the boring majority. Why? Because you're not thinking *different,* you're thinking *same.*

Microsoft and Apple have operating systems that allow you to run programs, edit videos, work formulas, surf the 'net, draft documents, etc. But if you're an Apple fan, you are likely to share Apple's values of style, individuality, creativity, and nonconformity. You'll likely consider their products intuitive, innovative, and attractive. Apple has gone to great lengths to cultivate those feelings and opinions by developing a visual and verbal language to effectively communicate with the consumer in its advertising and packaging. Many of its advertising messages in the 1990s and early 2000s focused on its products empowering creatives and original thinkers– people who didn't identify with the majority.

If you're not an Apple products' buyer, you probably think of yourself as rational, practical, and intellectual. You think Apple fans are easily duped into paying more for non-essential, designy fluff. You don't care much about Apple's superficial values because you have important work to do.

I emphasize the importance of emotion and relationships because I assume you've put in the hard work of making sure your product or service is awesome. But you should also know that it's highly likely that you have a competitor that offers a product or service with very similar customer benefits. What you must realize is that *how* you connect with your customers through the visual and verbal language that you use to express your company's personality (branding) will be the determining factor on whether or not they buy from you.

In the battle between brands, consumers choose sides based on the personality of the brands that they most resonate with. Don't let a competitor with an inferior product or service steal your business by doing a better job of connecting with those who should be your customers.

Assemble Your Brand Trust

As a business builder or entrepreneur, I can assume you are eager to tackle the challenge of building your brand. Start by assembling a brand development committee, a **brand trust** which should consist of no more than six individuals who will work with you on developing and executing your brand. Invite people you know and trust who have a feel for your personality and values if you are a sole proprietor, or the personality and values of your company. They could be senior-level employees who have been with the company for a long time, members of your advisory board, or the founder. It's very important to establish an environment where members of your **brand trust** can be candid and share their honest opinion. Any introverts in your group will likely be over shadowed by the extroverts, so make the effort to ensure you get everyone's thoughts and opinions or you'll end up with a biased result. If your **brand trust** consists of "me, myself and I," that's OK too. Schedule two or three hours with your **brand trust** in front of a whiteboard, have a plentiful supply of your favorite caffeinated beverages, then discuss your responses to the first four steps in the **brand strategy** discovery process (which you will learn about in Part II). Assemble your **brand trust** as often as needed until you have consensus. I often find it very productive to find a place off-site and away from the day-to-day distractions of running a business to stay focused and creative.

Depending on the number of people in your **brand trust**, expect to spend several days, or even a few weeks, on this process to let these new ideas marinate in your mind. If you are working solo, you might be able to move through the process over a few days, but make sure you still allow yourself time to get used to your brand image before you hit the 'all systems go' button.

Now that you have a far more comprehensive understanding of what a brand is, and the importance of creating an emotional connection with your customers, let's dive into some self-reflection with the first four steps of forging your **brand strategy**. This will lay the foundation that defines the personality of your company which we will use to create that solid, remarkable brand your company deserves.

PART II
FIRE up your Brand Strategy!

"Tactics without strategy is the noise before defeat."

-- Sun Tzu

What makes your business worthy of your customers' time and money? Who are your customers? Why should they care and how can they pick you out of a crowd? I will help you answer those questions using four steps that I will refer to using the acronym FIRE. The answers to the questions will ultimately create your **brand strategy**.

F – Find Your 'Brand Spark'

In order to be irreplaceable one must always be different."

– Coco Chanel

Unless you've invented a product that enables time travel, developed a pill to cure cancer, or are bottling water from the fountain of youth, your business has competitors that offer products or services similar to yours. The first step in developing your brand is to understand exactly *why* someone would buy your product or service from you. What makes it unique, different, or sets it apart? Some refer to this as your USP (unique selling point), but I prefer to call this your **brand spark** because it is the catalyst that will ignite the rest of your brand– what you say, how you say it, who you say it to, and where you say it.

When asking clients what makes them stand out from their competitors, most say something like: "It's our people," "It's our quality," "We provide the best service," or "We *really* care about our customers." Unfortunately, their competitors often say the same things, with a similar mistaken belief that these are USPs when, in reality, they are actually similarities.

Creating a **brand spark** on one of these **brand attributes** is VERY challenging because the terms describing these attributes have been overused and have lost their meaning. Just listen to the radio and it won't be long before you hear messages repeated over and over again in advertisements for companies whose quality and service isn't that great, and their actions show they don't really care that much about their customers. Consequently, your brand will get more attention and be more convincing if you develop a unique **brand spark** that will enhance your reputation with your great people, quality, service, and customer care.

Your **brand spark** can be something that already exists in your organization which has yet to be discovered, or it can be something you are passionate about and want to create for your brand. I will show you both methods, one for discovering a **brand spark** and one for creating it.

Method 1 - Discovery

Discovering your Brand Spark is the process of brainstorming attributes that exist in your company or product then mining those attributes for unique and compelling themes that will help you stand out from your competition. I'm going to explain the process first then I'll illustrate it using the story of Chuck Norris' CForce water brand.

Take Action

Step 1 : List Brand Attributes.

Read through this section before meeting with your **brand trust** in order to get a clear understanding of the process and terminology. Then gather your **brand trust** around a white board and list all the attributes you believe your company has that are unique to your industry. This could be where you are located, the unique materials you use, the processes you use, the unique benefits you offer, your value proposition, etc. These **brand attributes** should be written in a single word or short phrase.

Use the following questions to guide you:
1. Where did your product or service come from? Why was it invented/developed? Who invented/introduced it?
2. If you have a proprietary process or trademark, what is it?
3. What is remarkable or memorable about your company or product(s)?
4. What can you deliver at a consistently high level that you want your business to be known for?
5. What about your products or services is unique to your industry and important to your target customer?
6. Why do customers currently come to you instead of your competition?
7. What do customers love about your business? What do they tell their friends about your business?
8. What do your competitors envy about you, or what would you like your competitors to envy about you?
9. What do you want your customers to say after interacting with your brand that would be nearly impossible for them to say about your competitors?
10. How do you want people to feel about your company?

11. If you haven't launched your product or service yet, what is your competitive advantage?

Here are a few tips to consider in this brainstorming process.
- Remember not to dismiss any ideas or suggestions because one idea may lead to an even better idea.
- Also, consider incorporating solo work where members of your trust are asked to do some brainstorming on their own for a few minutes and then share what they've come up with. This provides an opportunity for your less vocal trust members to share their thoughts and opinions.
- Don't settle for superficial answers.
- When you run out of ideas take a mental break. Play Spikeball, roast a marshmallow, go for a walk, or have a snack before coming back to the list.

If you can't come up with any ideas that inspire you, skip to the next method and learn how to create your **brand spark**. When you feel you've exhausted all of your ideas, take a picture of your whiteboard and go to Step 2.

Step 2 : Identify Your Unique Brand Attributes.

Research your competitors' websites, trade magazine ads, and YouTube videos to determine what they claim as their key points of differentiation. What do they say to make them sound special? Do they have a unique process or product, is it their location, do they use a unique material, or do they adhere to a theme? If it's not obvious, it means that they don't know or aren't able to clearly communicate their key point(s) of difference. That bodes well for you because you're about to define yours.

Many brands I've consulted with have claimed that they are "true partners to their customers" or "service minded," that they "truly care about their customers," are "friendly," or "our people make the difference." If variations of these attributes show up on your list, ask yourselves if any of your competitors are saying the same things, whether you believe them to be true or not. If you choose a **brand spark** that is shared by a competitor, you need to be able to provide clear evidence to convince your customers to believe you. If you and your competitors share the "friendly" **brand spark**, you'll need to develop a message to convince your customers that your friendly business is friendlier than theirs.

Compare your competitors' **brand attributes** to the ones you've listed for your company. Circle **brand attributes** on your list that cannot be or are not currently promoted by any competitor. The **brand attributes** you circled have now made the shortlist for **brand spark** consideration.

Step 3: Rate Shortlist For Customer Relevance.

On a scale of 1-10, where 1 is negligible and 10 is highly significant, list each of your products' attributes and give them an appropriate score in relation to your most valuable customer. Your most valued customer is the type of person who is most likely to appreciate what makes your company different and who is willing to pay for that difference. They are usually characterized by gender, age, economic profile, employment, etc. We'll go into greater detail about identifying your core customer in the next chapter but for now, use your best guess.

Identify five or fewer of your highest-rated **brand attributes** and focus on them in Step 4 below.

Step 4 : Brainstorm Advertising Ideas for Each Attribute.

Spend fifteen minutes brainstorming advertising ideas for each of the top-rated **brand attributes** from Step 3.

The point of this exercise is to determine which **brand attribute** sparks prolific and exciting marketing and advertising ideas. You might consider inviting your marketing director, ad agency creative, or creative cousin to help you brainstorm ideas.

What would you put on a billboard?

What would a print ad look like?

What would a TV commercial or YouTube video look like?

Think about headlines, images, metaphors, and short storylines that you could use to clearly convey each brand attribute for the above formats.

If I owned a manufacturing plant and identified one of my top **brand attributes** was powered 100% by renewable energy, I would brainstorm advertising ideas commonly associated with a healthy environment. I might consider images like blue skies, mountain tops, clear streams, and meadows. And because I'm brainstorming and the sky's the limit, I might consider spokespeople who are well known in that industry who have strong associations with renewable energy. To save a little money, I could cast an attractive spokesperson with an outdoorsy look and get them to pose with my products or, better yet, show off our lack of waste.

Another idea is to call out my competitors with a comparison campaign to highlight how different we are. If I were designing a billboard, I could write a headline that reads, "We're most proud of what we don't produce." Then, underneath that comment I would have the word "US," below which I'd put a photo of white clouds floating in clear, blue skies. Under the word, "THEM" I'd use a picture of a sky filled with black smoke and smog.

Don't hold any ideas back because one idea will spark another. Do this for each of the top-rated **brand attributes** from Step 3.

The **brand attribute** that sparks the most ideas should be the top contender for **brand spark** consideration. Your **brand spark** will become the core element of your branding and marketing materials. Keep all the **brand attributes** that made your shortlist in your back pocket and use them whenever possible, but they should always take second stage to the **brand spark**.

Brand Discovery Example

Now that I've introduced you to the **brand spark** discovery method, I'd like to illustrate how it was used for Chuck Norris' bottled water company.

The story: Well diggers tapped an enormous artesian aquifer while drilling for an irrigation source to water the fields on Chuck Norris's home ranch in Navasota, Texas. The water was tested by hydrologists and found to be exceptionally pure with naturally high levels of essential minerals that gave the water a crisp flavor. The Norris' family decided to build a bottling plant across the street from their home and sell their water to the world, with proceeds going to their Kickstart Kids charity.

STEP 1: List the Company's Brand Attributes.

(For the purposes of this example, I've narrowed down CForce's **brand attributes** into a short list. Yours will likely be much longer.)

Attribute #1. The water is sourced from a sustainable artesian aquifer.

Attribute #2 The source is located in Navasota, Texas.

Attribute #3 "The water is very pure."

Attribute #4 The water is Chuck Norris' water.

Attribute #5 Proceeds go to the Kickstart Kids charity.

STEP 2: Identify the Company's <u>Unique</u> Brand Attributes.

Attribute #1: The water is sourced from a sustainable artesian aquifer.

Whoop-de-do. Bottled water comes from a variety of sources like rain, glaciers, springs, aquifers, and streams but no one seems to care. This attribute is not very unique and certainly not a key point to build a brand on, but it should be included in its marketing messages after leading with the **brand spark**.

Strike a line through this brand attribute.

Attribute #2: The source is located in Navasota, Texas.

Texas conjures images of whiskered cowboys and hot dusty plains, not a cool oasis of clear drinking water. It would be incredibly difficult to compete with brands that use refreshing images of glacier run-off, mountain springs, or even lush Fijian foliage to highlight their sources.

Strike a line through it.

Attribute #3: "The water is very pure."

Water purity is very, very important to anyone who drinks bottled water. It's almost always packaged in clear containers to show customers that there aren't any floaties, suspendies, or sinkies in the water. (Those are super gross!) All bottled water is purified, but CForce comes naturally pure with high mineral content, directly from the source.

Circle this attribute.

Attribute #4: The water was discovered on Chuck Norris' ranch.

No other water company can claim an authentic association with Chuck Norris.

Circle it.

Attribute #5: Proceeds go to Kickstart Kids.

Chuck Norris is passionate about Kickstart Kids, a charitable youth program he founded to help underprivileged kids through the discipline of Karate. Chuck and Gena Norris made the decision to bottle and sell the water for the sole purpose of creating a long-lasting source of revenue for Kickstart Kids. There will never be a time when proceeds of CForce do not benefit Kickstart Kids.

This is unique and should be circled.

STEP 3: Rate the circled attributes for customer relevance.

After identifying the most important **brand attributes**, which are "water purity," "Chuck Norris," and "Kickstart Kids," we prioritized them based on customer appeal and importance.

Water Purity: When speaking in front of large groups, I will often share the CForce story and ask the audience if water purity is important to them. I ask those with raised hands if any of them can tell me the amount of total dissolved solids (TDS) in their favorite bottled water. What usually follows is laughter because no one reads the label for TDS content. (Except for the time when there was one guy who actually worked for a bottled water company. That was embarrassing.)

I surmised that although water purity is important to consumers, my small focus groups would suggest that all bottled water is pure enough.

I would have rated this brand attribute 5 out of 10.

Chuck Norris: Chuck is one of the most famous tough-guy action stars in the world, especially among GenX and baby boomers, thanks to his movie roles as Lone Wolf McQuade and as Walker in the Walker Texas Ranger television series. He also has serious clout among Karate fans as a six-time undefeated World Professional  Middleweight Karate Champion. And if that's not enough, he has a cult following among high school and college students due to ridiculous, share-worthy Chuck Norris "facts" such as *"Chuck Norris' tears cure cancer, unfortunately he has never cried. Chuck Norris can kill two stones* *with one bird. When Chuck Norris slices onions, onions cry."* There are hundreds of these little gems, but it is obvious that Chuck Norris is sufficiently popular and interesting enough among a wide spectrum of potential customers to receive a rating of 10 out of 10.

Affiliation with Kickstart Kids: People like to do business with organizations that give back to the community, even if they don't recognize the charity, especially among younger consumers who appreciate corporate giving more than GenX and baby boomers.

I would have rated this brand attribute 6 out of 10.

STEP 4 – Brainstorm Advertising Ideas for the Top Contenders.

For the purposes of this example, I'll share some of the ideas I brainstormed for all three of our circled **brand attributes**. The brand attribute that created the most excitement was given a trophy and awarded the title: **brand spark**! The other ideas were given participation trophies because I didn't want them to feel bad. They are still frequently used whenever the occasion calls for them, so its not all bad for them!

Water Purity: Water purity conjures up images of crystal-clear mountain streams, lush foliage, and melting glaciers. I can also imagine a white, sterile laboratory with scientists in long lab coats working with glass tubes and testing equipment. "Pure. Powerful. Perfect." would be a great tagline. When the product launches, we could run a billboard with the words, "Purity has arrived" superimposed over a photo of the product. There aren't many original ideas from competitors focusing on the purity brand attribute.

Affiliation with Kickstart Kids: Showing kids working up a thirst, kicking, punching, and breaking boards, then drinking

CForce water would be real fun, but without Chuck being involved in these ads they would fall a little flat.

Which is why we should move on to evaluate the Chuck Norris brand attribute.

Chuck Norris: We could have Chuck Norris stare menacingly at the ground until the earth surrenders its water. We could create fun, new Chuck Norris facts about water and put them on the underside of the bottle caps. We could have Chuck Norris drink CForce and do some cool Karate stuff to make it look like it empowered him. We could make cool t-shirts and hats that suggest drinking CForce gives you Chuck Norris' powers. Imagine a billboard that showed Chuck Norris with a menacing expression while holding a bottle of CForce, with a headline that reads, "Put thirst in a chokehold." or "Punch thirst in the throat." We could even have Chuck Norris interacting with Kickstart Kids or talking about the water's purity to highlight those important attributes.

Assessment

Images of water purity are commonplace in the bottled water industry and showing pictures or a video of hydrologists in a science lab doesn't feel refreshing or appealing. While natural purity may not be worthy of a **brand spark**, it's a product feature that ought to be included in some marketing messages.

Kickstart Kids doesn't have nearly the broad customer appeal or widespread awareness of Chuck Norris. While it may not be worthy of a **brand spark**, it's a point of differentiation that ought to be mentioned in most marketing messages.

And the winner is… Chuck Norris!

The brand attribute with the most exciting and prolific ideas hit like a karate punch to the solar plexus –Chuck Norris sparks a variety of marketing and advertising ideas. He should be the **brand spark**. The CForce brand should lead with Chuck Norris images and personality to create initial interest and then leverage that initial interest to introduce messages on water purity and the brand's affiliation with Kickstart Kids.

Before I started consulting with CForce, the brand was centered on purity. Their ads, billboards, website, and packaging focused on its unusual, natural purity. Chuck's wife Gena, CForce's CEO and Founder, is uncommonly health conscious. She watches everything she eats and drinks and avoids anything that might have a whisper of unhealthiness, so water purity is extremely important to her. Her personal values strongly influenced the initial decision to focus branding on purity. Unfortunately, their product wasn't generating the excitement it deserved.

After going through this brand discovery process, she and her executive team came to appreciate the value of the Chuck Norris action star persona. As a result, CForce made the decision to make Chuck Norris the **brand spark**. The label and case packaging were revised to include an illustration of Chuck Norris, and his image is used in all of its marketing and advertising messages. Was it successful? Heck! Which billboard would most interest you in trying CForce?

Method 2-Creating your Brand Spark

If you really can't discover something unique and remarkable about your business that inspires great advertising ideas, you'll need to create your **brand spark**!

You can build a brand on anything that you are passionate about!

Passions and interests inspire words, images, and phrases that can then be parlayed very tastefully into a business brand. For example, golf is a passion that inspires words, images, and phrases like hole-in-one, fore!, birdie, par, marker, caddie, clubs, tee, golf ball, hazard, green, clubhouse, fairway, putter, and rough, etc. These golf elements can inspire colors, patterns, textures, and materials that can be used for interior and exterior design, websites, advertising campaigns, packaging, and more.

Topgolf is a restaurant and entertainment chain with dozens of locations across America and several outlets in countries throughout the world. Topgolf is a great example that demonstrates passions can be used as **brand sparks**.

If you and your team share the same passion, you're likely to have a strong visual and verbal vocabulary to draw from.

The process of creating a **brand spark** for your company begins with the questions: "What am I passionate about? What brings me joy and captivates my dreams?" These passions can be catalysts for creating a remarkable brand. You'll be looking for passions that inspire a unique look, feel, and personality for your business.

Take Action

STEP 1: Brand Trust... ASSEMBLE!

Assemble your **brand trust** in front of a white board when everyone is filled with energy and ideas, so avoid scheduling your meeting after lunch when people tend to be lethargic. Consider taking a brisk walk with your team, climbing stairs, doing push ups, sipping caffeine or anything else to get blood to your brain before your meeting starts.

STEP 2: Brainstorm Your Passions

Explain that a brand can be inspired by one of their passions or interests and you need their help sharing their personal favorites.

(It's important to have a deep love and commitment that generates that passion as, for it to become a part of your brand, it will need all the energy you have to sustain and defend it.)

Hand out a pen and a pad of sticky notes to each member of the **brand trust** and give them 10-15 minutes to write down as many of their passions as they can. Have them use one sticky note for each idea.

STEP 3: Passion Presentation

Invite each of your members to post their ideas on the whiteboard and explain their ideas to the group. After each person has presented their passions, write down any new passions that come up in the discussion. Ask the group which ideas sound most interesting and why.

STEP 4: Vote

Now that you have explored everyone's passions, it's time to narrow down the list to the top two. Give each person three sticky notes and have them write down on individual notes a passion they find most appealing and then ask them to place their choices on a separate area of the whiteboard. Add up the passions with the most votes and continue the voting process until you have two finalists. Then move on to Step 5.

STEP 5: Brainstorm Words, Images, and Phrases Associated with the Chosen Passions

Take a picture of the whiteboard covered in sticky notes to keep a record of your ideas, then clear it off. Draw a line down the center and write down each of the two passions on either side at the top of the board. Then take a few minutes to brainstorm the words, images, and phrases associated with each of them, like we did for golf a page or two ago. These ideas will become the ingredients and inspiration for your potential new brand.

STEP 6: Brainstorm Advertising Ideas for Each Attribute.

What passion-inspired images and metaphors can you use in your advertising and marketing messages that will help your company stand apart from your competitors in such an interesting way that it's certain to get people talking? Refer to the two individual lists you previously created on the whiteboard and spend 20 to 30 minutes brainstorming advertising ideas for each of the two passions you are focusing on. You may want to invite the most creative people you know to participate in this exercise.

Conjure headlines, images, metaphors, and short storylines for a billboard, print ad, TV commercial or YouTube video. List them on the board. The passion that sparks the most prolific and exciting marketing and advertising ideas should be crowned the **brand spark**!

I followed this **brand creation method** to develop an adventurous **brand spark** for Maverik convenience stores. I grew up with Maverik Country Stores. They were well known as an old-fashioned, cowboy-themed convenience store chain inspired by western television and cowboy movies popular in the 1960's. Maverik stores were known for fresh baked food, "sammiches," and inexpensive gas. Their stores looked like saloons. They even had hitchin' posts out front. After decades of hard riding, Maverik developed a reputation for cheap food and low-quality fuel.

In 2001 their new VP of Marketing believed the sun was setting on the tired, old, western branding and was eager to breathe life into a new iteration.

There was very little about the company that inspired great marketing ideas. The **brand attributes** that we identified were 'independence' and 'excitement'. We knew we needed to express that spirit in whatever brand we created. But where to start? We conducted informal interviews with customers to discover what made them excited to go to a Maverik convenience store. We learned that people typically didn't like going to gas stations. It was a necessary evil. But we also found that people most enjoyed going to convenience stores when they were on their way fishing, hunting, snowmobiling, mountain biking, skiing, snowboarding, etc. They gave themselves permission to buy drinks and snacks for the road while they filled their cars with fuel. They associated the eager anticipation of adventure with their visit to the convenience store.

Adventure was the shared passion.

It was easy to brainstorm words, phrases, and images centered on the passion of adventure. And it didn't take long for my creative team and myself to brainstorm ideas for advertising filtered through the lens of adventure. We even came up with a new tagline to replace Country Stores – *Adventure's First Stop*. We positioned Maverik as *the* place people go to start adventures. (Even if an adventure is work or soccer practice.)

Summary

You can discover your **brand spark** from a brand attribute that already exists in your company or create one from a passion that inspires you or your executive team. Either method will help you establish the one thing that makes your business stand apart from your competition. It will become the focal point of all of your messages and spark the look, feel and personality of your brand.

If you haven't already downloaded your *Ignite Your Brand* workbook from https://ernburn.com/kindling, do it now while you have the time. Then, take a moment and write down your **brand spark** in the Find Your Brand Spark section.

With your **brand spark** identified, your next step is to identify the ideal customer profile most likely to buy what you're selling. If you don't know exactly who your target customer is, you'll spread your resources too thin as you create products, programs, and marketing campaigns to reach the unreachable "everyone." When you know who your core customer is, it becomes easy to develop the products they want, the messages that will attract them, and find the avenues most likely to reach them. So, who is your target customer?

I – Identify Your Target Customer

"Everyone is not your customer."

– Seth Godin

A company I consulted with (that will remain confidential) developed online software that enables small businesses to manage the sales and informational media messages that they broadcast on their lobby and retail outlet TV displays. One of the company product features integrates with popular social media platforms, making it easy for the small business to post content to its social media pages. This means a small business that doesn't have brick and mortar stores where customers wait *could* use the software to promote their products and services on social media. My client expressed the desire to target small business owners that have retail space *and* small business owners that do not. Targeting two different customer types would require my client to spend a lot of time and money conducting two separate marketing campaigns because both customer groups do not share the same set of challenges. Small business owners that do not have retail locations wouldn't care about the primary product benefit of educating and selling to waiting customers.

Your **target customer** is the group of the population most likely to appreciate your **brand spark**, recognize the need for your product or service, and pay for it. They spend more money and shop more frequently for products and services like yours than any other customer segment. The more you can identify shared attributes of your target customers, the easier it will be to craft the branding elements that will attract and excite them. It's also easier to place those messages in the right marketing channels where they are more likely to be seen by the right people.

Your target customers congregate with those who share similar tastes, personalities, interests and values. This means they swim together. They follow the same social media influencers, watch the same movies and videos, are interested in the same sports, listen to similar music, and gather at the same venues.

Cast the right-sized net.

Don't fall for the temptation to get distracted by potential customers who could *possibly* be convinced to buy your products or services. You'll have to spend many-times the hours and money to reach them. Your secondary customers are more likely to become aware of your product(s) or service(s) through the customers you target directly, and existing customers.

Most executives cringe at the notion of excluding anyone from their target customer demographic. They want their brand to appeal to the widest customer base possible. They want to market to everyone that might possibly buy their product or service. However, there is a critical difference between the way the marketing department and sales department should focus on customers. The marketing department should focus on those most likely to pay for your product or service, the sales department should sell to anyone willing to buy.

And here's the reason: Trying to appeal to a wide range of customers with diverse interests, tastes and values requires advertising messages to be toned down in order to reduce the possibility of offending someone. As a result, those advertising messages lack punch and potency. They contribute to the unremarkable, flavorless noise your business must rise above in order to get the attention of your most likely customers. It's kind of like fishing – you need to know what you're fishing for so you can use tackle that works.

Casting a wide net is also very expensive. Regardless of your preferred advertising media, you'll pay for every click or impression. So, don't waste your money advertising to people who are not likely to become customers.

Organizations that are unwilling to identify a highly specific target customer don't have the focus and discipline to fashion a brand image and voice that is enticing and sufficiently different to cut through the incessant fog of advertising to penetrate the hearts of their potential customers. This is super important, so I'll say it again. If you're not willing to focus on a highly specific customer type, you won't have the focus and discipline to create an image and **brand personality** that is enticing enough and different enough to cut through the din of other advertising to get noticed. If your message is for everyone, you'll connect with no one.

How to identify your core customers.

Regardless of what business you're in, there is usually one but sometimes two types of customer that bring in the majority of your revenue. The next chapter outlines the steps to identify these target customers.

 *Take Action*

STEP 1: List the Characteristics of Your Best Customers.

Your best customers are going to share similar attributes. It might be income, type of work, hobbies, interests, faith, education, location, gender, race, etc. If your company has been in business for a while, ask the person in charge of sales to print out a list of current customers and identify the top 10-20% that contribute significantly to your company revenue. If you are just starting your business and don't already have customers, follow my suggestions below to list the characteristics and demographics you think your customers will share - these will become your customer profile. It may not be perfect, but you can always update your customer profile as you grow.

Assemble your **brand trust** in front of a whiteboard with plenty of caffeinated beverages for everyone and identify the most common shared attributes of your target demographic. Here is a list of questions to get you started.

1. What percentage of your best customers are male and what percentage are female?
2. What is their average age?
3. Do the majority have in common - hobbies, interests, income, faith, race, politics, etc.?
4. What are their occupations?
5. What websites or social media influencers do they follow? What social media channels do the majority spend time on? Do they read the paper, watch TV, listen to the radio, listen to ad-free internet radio, watch YouTube videos, play community soccer, go to professional football games, go to the orchestra, donate to charities, etc.?

Here are a handful of interests, hobbies, and demographics to jumpstart your ideas

Interests
- Art/antiques
- Cycling/running
- Camping
- Dieting
- Crafts
- Foreign travel
- Fine dining
- Fast food
- Coin/stamp collecting
- DIY/workshop
- Recreational vehicles
- Health foods/vitamins
- Business opportunities
- YouTube browsing
- Book reading
- Fashion/clothing
- Bible/devotional reading
- Physical fitness/exercise
- Online subscription music
- Sweepstakes
- Sewing
- Needlework/knitting
- Gardening
- Wildlife/environmental issues
- Self-improvement
- Watching sports on TV
- Watching sports online
- Charities/volunteer work

Demographics
- Annual income
- Gender
- Nationality
- Age
- Zip code
- Educational level
- Marital status

You are likely to identify a handful of customer types and it's important to recognize each type so you can create an intentional marketing strategy to directly address each one. You don't need to invest time or money creating marketing strategies for every customer type, but it's still important to recognize their value so you can determine which type you should focus on and, more importantly, which ones you shouldn't. Focus on one or two customer types that will likely buy from you and who may also make purchases more frequently than the others.

Allow me to use my experience at Maverik as an example.

Maverik sells fuel, freshly made food, snacks and beverages to men, women and children of all ages, and economic and ethnic backgrounds, but through careful observation at predefined locations they were able to group consumers into nine profiles based on what they bought, their estimated age, gender, and perceived occupation. Maverik was able to associate a financial value to each group based on what they purchased and how frequently they made purchases.

The customer type that shopped most frequently and made large purchases of products with high profit margins were men between the ages of 18-45 with blue-collar jobs. They drove trucks and used gas-powered equipment, so they bought a lot of fuel. These guys were not salad-eating, low-carb dieters. They traveled together in crews, were physically active, and worked up serious appetites for high-calorie food, snacks, energy drinks, coffee, and sodas found in convenience stores. We also found that this group included a high percentage of Hispanics.

After identifying your core customer types, it's extremely useful to translate them into something more relatable and personal than: "Blue Collar Workers" or "Millennial Women with Children."

STEP 2: Create A Buyer Persona for Each Group.

Buyer personas are fictional composite characters that reflect the key attributes of your audience and are an excellent way to visualize target customers as individuals instead of faceless people in a crowd.

Use the general customer information you've identified or determined to create a description of each customer group as if they were an individual. Give each persona a name and include their age, gender, interests, income, family, and any other details that will help you and others better understand their behavior. Find a photo on the internet that best represents the persona as well, and it won't be long before you start thinking of your customers as individuals. It will look and feel stereotypical, but you aren't using this to judge people, you're using it to help you focus on the individual customer.

If I were to create a persona that Maverik might target, it might read like this:

Jeremy Martinez

Male, age 24

Second-generation American. Parents are from Mexico.

He works with his friend's and cousin at his dad's landscaping business.

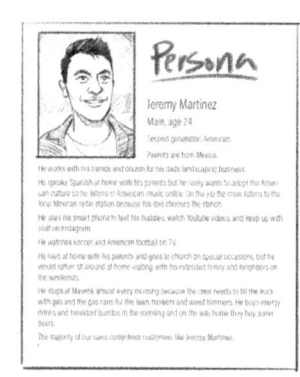

He speaks Spanish at home with his parents, but he says he really wants to adopt the broader, national culture of America, so he listens to popular music online. The crew listens to the local Latino radio station when on the job because his dad chooses the station.

He uses his smartphone to text his buddies, watch YouTube videos, and to keep up with stuff on Instagram.

He watches soccer and American football on TV.

He lives at home with his parents and goes to church on special occasions, but he prefers to stay home on the weekends and visit with his extended family and neighbors.

He stops at Maverik almost every morning because the crew needs to fill the truck and containers for the lawn mower and weed trimmers with gas. He buys energy drinks and breakfast burritos in the morning, and on the way home he and the crew buy beer.

A large percentage of sales come from customers like Jeremy Martinez.

Create a persona like this for each of your customer groups. Post the personas in order of importance on a wall where everyone can see so they are always in the forefront of your mind. As a leadership team, decide which of the customer segments you are going to focus on in your marketing strategy so when someone says, "Hey! My mom would hate this ad," you can say, "Is your mom a Jeremy Martinez? If we created a campaign that your mom liked, then Jeremy would probably hate it!"

Take a moment and write down the definition of your target customer in your *Ignite Your Brand* workbook.

Summary

Defining your target customer may have been one of the hardest things you've ever done. If you completed this section and have a description of your target customer or have crafted a customer persona or two, you've given your company invaluable FOCUS! You and everyone else in the company know exactly *who* you serve. And knowing who your target customers are will help influence the choice of products you offer them, the visual and verbal language you'll craft to attract them, and the media channels you'll use to reach them.

Now that you've identified your target customers, it's time to turn your business into a religion. Can I get an amen?!

R – Realize Your Core Belief

People don't buy what you do; they buy why you do it. And what you do simply proves what you believe.

– **Simon Sinek,** TED Talk phenom, author, and speaker.

I enjoy competitive sports, and in 2012 I found myself watching Michael Phelps swim in the Summer Olympics. He was crushing world records and he made it look easy. After winning each individual race, he would set his enormous jaw, clench his fist, and act as though it was all part of the plan. My reaction? "Meh." If it wasn't a big deal to him, it wasn't a big deal to me.

Then there was the medley race. In the final laps, Michael was pounding on the swimming platform and screaming with his teammates at the top of his lungs. I was off my sofa with the rest of the world pounding on pillows and screaming in concert. When the final swimmer touched the wall, the team went berserk!! Their enthusiasm was contagious. I went crazy with them and so did millions of Americans.

We become passionate when we're invited to share the passions and beliefs of others.

What is a Core Belief?

Your **brand spark** is the uniqueness you bring to the world. Your **core belief** is the reason why you do it. The **core belief** you have in your company's role in the world will influence the language, tone, and the visual elements you choose in advertising and marketing to convey your **brand spark** in a very authentic way. And until you identify and document your **core belief** in your **brand strategy** and share it with those who work for you or with you, they will make decisions or recommendations based on their own beliefs, which may conflict with yours.

Typically, businesses begin when the founder sees a need for something new. They may have discovered a business opportunity, but it's a **core belief** about that opportunity that motivates them to make an investment in time, energy, and money to make it a reality. It could be a belief in conserving resources, improving well-being, reducing fatigue, etc. Shared beliefs in the important role the company plays in the world sustains dedication and effort from the company's employees and creates lasting customer loyalty.

It's been my experience that many CEOs have trained themselves to shy away from emotion in order to maintain a logical and pragmatic demeanor. Consequently, it's often difficult for them to put a finger on their emotional motivations. This is detrimental to company morale and the heart of the brand because employees want to follow a leader with a purpose. It's essential that they understand the CEO's personal motivation above and beyond turning a profit. Unless it is expressed and clearly understood, the potential for friction between the owner/CEO and employees is high. If everyone isn't rowing in the same direction, everyone gets exhausted going nowhere.

Clearly expressing your company's core belief also creates an emotional connection with your customers. When you do, individuals that share your belief will be drawn to you and your business.

One of the greatest global brands was founded on a belief that time was a valuable commodity and shouldn't be wasted. Its belief was so powerful that it inspired a whole new industry.

Prior to 1948, people who went out to eat would drive to a restaurant, wait to be seated, wait to have their order taken, then wait for their order to be prepared by the kitchen and then delivered to their table. They did a lot of waiting.

Brothers Richard (Dick) and Maurice (Mac) McDonald saw an opportunity to streamline meal production in an assembly-line fashion to dramatically reduce the wait time which was accepted back then when dining out. They called it the "Speedee Service System" now commonly known as "fast food." Customers would place an order for food that was already being prepared and cooked in the kitchen and would then pick it up at another window within just a few minutes. It was revolutionary! That **core belief** became the **brand spark** that caught milkshake equipment salesman, Ray Kroc's eye, who then turned McDonald's into a global franchise. The McDonald brothers' passion for constant process innovation to save time suggests they believed time was a valuable commodity and shouldn't be wasted. The billions of people that came to McDonald's was evidence that there were plenty of customers who shared that belief.

Dick and Mac may not have articulated their **core belief** into an employee training manual or brand standards guide, but their daily involvement and high standards served them well as a small business. Today it wouldn't be surprising to learn that McDonald's best leaders, employees, and partners share the **core belief** that time is a valuable commodity and shouldn't be wasted. It certainly attracts customers with the same core value.

Realize Your Core Belief

 *Take Action*

STEP 1: Probe for Your Core Belief

I've learned from experience that being able to express your **core belief** without coaching can be very challenging, so I've designed a series of questions to help you discover it. All of these questions are different means to the same end. You don't need to answer them all to achieve the objective, but I encourage you to do your best because each will force you to approach the topic from different angles. The answers will shed light on your business beliefs.

Write down the answers to these questions in the Realize Your Core Belief section in your *Ignite Your Brand* workbook.

1. Do you have a mantra you frequently reference or repeat? If you do, there is probably something you believe that drives it. Why is that mantra important to you?
2. What do you believe about your industry or about your role in that industry that drives you to do your best?

3. Other than making a profit, why are you in business?
4. Other than earning wages, why do your employees bring their best efforts to work for you?
5. Is there something about your process that saves time, money, or resources? What exactly is it, as it would suggest you have a strong belief in it?
6. Why would anyone care about your **brand spark**?

STEP 2: Write it Down

Take a look at your answers. You should be able to identify a common theme. Make a couple attempts to write down your company's **core belief** in one or two short sentences. Begin with, "We at (insert the name of your company) believe (fill in the blank.)" It should stir some passion inside you! When you have a few ideas that you like, share them with your **brand trust** to see if they ring true to them. The actual process of vocalizing your **core belief** in a presentation is another test of its authenticity. When you hear it coming out of your mouth, you'll either cringe or get goose bumps.

When you feel deep in your soul that you've nailed it, make it public. Introduce that **core belief** during new employee orientations, put it on your website, post it in a common area in your business and measure your strategies against it. Do everything you can to demonstrate that you live by your **core belief,** especially if it's inconvenient or comes at a financial cost, because that's when it's measured most. When you make this level of commitment, it will attract those employees and customers that share your beliefs. It will also guide your advertising and marketing messages. When you measure your decisions against your **core belief,** you'll always measure up.

If you hit a roadblock, come back to this step later. Lightning will strike while you take a shower, take a walk, or slip into that happy, fuzzy zone before falling asleep.

Veg out with me.

To illustrate the type of **core beliefs** we are looking for, let's use a fictitious company called Veg-Pat-E, Inc., that manufactures vegetable-based hamburger patties. The fact that it produces a product  as a substitute for red meat would suggest that the business' **core belief** is something like: "We believe a veggie-based diet will lead people to healthier and happier lives," or: "We believe the business of raising and slaughtering animals for food is inhumane and environmentally irresponsible."

Either **core belief** would influence branding decisions like colors, imagery, sponsorships, and charitable giving.

Choosing green or blue would be better than anything on the red spectrum which could suggest blood or red meat. It would be a good idea to use images of vegetable crops or a cornucopia of vegetables and avoid pictures of cows or cattle. When considering event sponsorships or charitable giving, Veg-Pat-E would avoid rodeos at all costs, favoring healthy eating initiatives or environmental awareness programs.

Under your effective leadership, your **core belief** will strongly influence every aspect of the company. But it needs to be authentic. The temptation to save time or money at the expense of brand integrity can sabotage your company's reputation. For example: if your brand has a **core belief** in environmental responsibility but decides to save money by purchasing plastic utensils instead of recycled paper utensils, loyal customers who share your beliefs will take personal offense.

If your **core belief** doesn't truly live in your heart and in the hearts of your business leaders, it won't have the energy required to sustain it. Employees and customers will quickly see through it and see that you lack integrity, which will do more harm than good.

Your **core belief** is also valuable as a catalyst that can inspire you and your employees, while also giving your customers one more thing to love about you.

Defining your **core belief** is one of the hardest **brand attributes** to define because it's not a scientific equation that has only one answer. However, when you do define it, your **core belief** will serve as a catalyst to inspire the right actions for your company every day.

You have **F**-ound your **brand spark**, **I**-dentified your target customers, and **R**-ealized your **core belief**, now let's move on to the final step of lighting your brand on FIRE by **E**-xplaining your brand adjectives.

E – Establish Your Brand Adjectives

You're either gonna define yourself, for yourself, or you're gonna let somebody else define you.

– **Gary Vaynerchuck**

How do your customers describe your brand?

What vehicle brand is safe, conservative, sturdy, and reliable? What beer brand is mysterious, exotic, exciting, and premium? What smartphone brand is creative, life-stylish, intuitive, and fun? What soft drink brand is all-American, original, refreshing, and happy?

Volvo, Dos Equis, Apple, and Coca Cola can easily be recognized by those adjectives because they've been used consistently and intentionally in their advertising messages. They have a distinctive voice. They know who they are and have documented how their brand should be represented in their **Brand Bible**, which helps everyone who works on the brand to do things consistently, to thus reinforce it in the minds of their customers.

There is a distinction between **brand attributes** and brand adjectives. **Brand attributes** describe the physical elements of the brand. (Size, location, processes, materials, services, etc.) Brand adjectives describe the personality of the brand. (conservative, fun, sophisticated, serious, playful, etc.) The adjectives you use to describe your brand will provide valuable guidance in selecting branding assets (pictures, fonts, colors, patterns, textures, vocabulary, etc.) that you will use in your advertising messages. I'll show you how to select those assets in Part III.

In this step, you'll select five or six adjectives to describe the brand you want to be. At least two of those adjectives should not describe or be applicable to any of your competitors. In fact, the fewer descriptors you have in common with your competitors the better, because if your brand can be described with the same adjectives that describe your competitors, there really isn't that much difference, is there? The purpose of this exercise is to create a difference that helps you express what makes you unique.

To assist you in this exciting adventure of adjective hunting, I'll lead you through the process of harvesting adjectives for your consideration by referencing "Aspirational Brands." We'll then have some fun testing the adjectives you selected in a role-playing exercise called "The Desired Customer Reaction" and wrap up this section by introducing the **brand matrix**– a nifty tool I invented to help remove the guesswork and subjectivity of determining what's on-brand or off-brand.

Aspirational Brands

One of the easiest ways to choose your brand descriptors is to be inspired by your favorite brands. These brands have made an emotional connection with you which is why you like them. And because you like them, it will be very easy for you to describe them.

 *Take Action*

STEP 1: Share The Brands You Aspire to be Like

Get together with your **brand trust** and have each member list 3-5 of their favorite brands they would like your company to look and feel like. Look at brands outside of your industry. What brands attract and excite you? What brands would you like your business to look and feel like?

Don't worry if members of your trust choose some of the same brands. That's actually a very good sign.

STEP 2: List the Adjectives and Define

DISNEY	HALLMARK	INTUIT	MONSTER
family-friendly	emotional	intelligent	urban
exciting	sensitive	clean	exciting
happy	warm	intuitive	dangerous
optimistic	heartfelt	friendly	aggressive
positive	sincere		edgy
wholesome			gritty
bright			
bold			

Next to each brand, list 3-7 adjectives that the member would use to describe them. Your list should be inspired by something like this, but with the brands of your choice:

Add any adjectives that describe your company which haven't been mentioned.

When each member of your **brand trust** goes through this exercise, you will likely discover certain adjectives mentioned repeatedly. These are the adjectives you'll want to focus on. Circle all the adjectives that you want your company to embody.

STEP 3: Condense and Define Your Selected Adjectives

As you go through this exercise, you'll realize some of the adjectives will be very similar, yet not all members of your brand trust will interpret the same adjectives in the same way. For example, 'cool' could mean frosty and aloof, or it could mean trendy, highly acceptable, and fashionable. In order to evaluate their potential inclusion in your brand, each member of the **brand trust** needs to have the same understanding of the adjectives.

Take a moment as a group to decide which adjectives are similar, then assign definitions for each of the adjectives you circled in R- Realize Your Core Belief.

STEP 4: Select The Top Five or Six

As a group, pare down your list of favorite adjectives to five or six that best describe the brand you want yours to be. Include their definitions. Make sure at least two of the adjectives do not apply to your competitors' brands, if not, your customers will have a hard time seeing or feeling the difference between you and your competitor(s).

Write your adjectives down in the section Establish Your Brand Adjectives in your *Ignite Your Brand* workbook. You're going to use them in Part III to select colors, textures, fonts, images, and other branding elements that use the same adjectives to describe them.

Test your adjectives by experimenting with them in The Desired Customer Reaction exercise below.

 *Take Action*

The Desired Customer Reaction

What do you want your target customers to say after seeing or hearing an advertisement, browsing your website, making a purchase in person or online, receiving a thank-you note, using your app, reading something your company posted on social media, seeing your logo at a sponsored event or sports arena, or recognizing a donation to a charity?

Customer endorsements and referrals are the most effective marketing tool, so it's in your company's best interest to orchestrate experiences across all customer touch points in such a remarkable way that it literally elicits a specific desired vocal reaction, such as: "Wow, (insert your company's name) was really (insert desired adjective)!"

If you want your target customers to say, "Wow, (your business name) is exciting!," would you paint the walls of your offices egg-shell white, hang landscape paintings on the wall, install beige carpet, and have a dress code of khakis and golf shirts? Definitely not exciting.

I found that it helps executives getter a clearer vision of how they want their company to be described if I paint a visual picture of their customers by getting out of my seat and assuming the target customer's character. I use exaggerated mannerisms, voice, and language while pantomiming a reaction to a brand experience such as walking out of a retail location, receiving a text message, or opening an email.

In one such performance for a convenience store chain, I channeled my inner "Bubba" with a bold swagger and broad shoulders. While pantomiming my exit from the store I turned to my invisible buddies (notice I didn't say *besties or BFF's. Wrong crowd,*) and said, "Hey dudes, that place rocked!" Yes. That's something Bubba would say and it's a feeling that he would desire. Things that rock are a good thing for Bubba.

I repeated the same actions but used the phrase "Wow, that store was gorgeous!" Everyone knows right away if the phrase resonates or feels natural for their customer when they hear and see it in action.

Watching me offer suggestions is both entertaining and enlightening, but my point is that you should try it. You'll be surprised at the level of clarity you'll experience as you hear the words of your customer come out of your mouth.

Write down your Desired Customer Reaction in your *Ignite Your Brand* workbook for easy reference.

Use your Desired Customer Reaction to guide the selection of your website design, interior/exterior building design, uniforms, dress code, language, and image decisions. Ask yourself, "Would (insert idea you are considering) elicit (desired customer reaction)?" If not, consider an alternative that would. Otherwise, your customers are going to receive mixed signals from you.

The Brand Matrix

Another great tool to communicate the personality of your brand is to establish a **brand matrix.**

Each of your business departments needs to make decisions every day.

"What should we use for employee uniforms?"

"What colors, fonts, and design elements should we use for our website?"

"What kinds of products should we develop and what should we call them?"

"What charities or events should we sponsor?"

"What theme should we use for this year's trade show?"

"What should the lighting fixtures look like?"

"What should the ad look like?"

And the list never ends. How does a person evaluate those decisions to strengthen the brand in a way that isn't biased to their own personal interpretations? Personal interpretations of what is considered "on-brand" are as diverse as the individuals working on the brand, and not every idea can be clearly divided between "totally on-brand" and "totally off-brand." So, I've often found it helpful to develop a **brand matrix** to assist employees and third-party partners in evaluating ideas that will best strengthen the brand.

A **brand matrix** is a graph that uses your brand adjectives to help you evaluate your ideas to determine if they are more or less on-brand.

Take Action

Create Your Brand Matrix

Divide your list of brand adjectives into two separate themes based on what they have in common. On a piece of paper or on a whiteboard, draw a large rectangle and write one of your themes on the top and write the second theme on the right-hand side. Put your logo in the top right corner. Ideas that you are considering should be placed on the matrix by how closely they are associated with each theme. The more your idea is associated with each theme, the closer it should be placed to your logo and the more on-brand it is.

Let's use the Maverik convenience store brand as an example.

The adjectives that could describe Maverik's brand are: thrilling (heart racing), extreme (a little dangerous), off the beaten path (unexpected and unique/outdoors), and adventurous (a sense of adventure, away from the norm).

I grouped the adjectives into two major themes: **Intensity** (thrilling, extreme, unexpected) and **Setting** (off the beaten path, adventurous).

I drew a graph that looked like this:

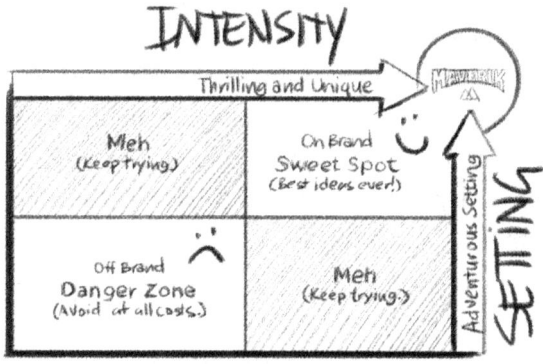

Ideas being considered for anything, including marketing, advertising, packaging, construction, sponsorships, events, etc., would be placed on the matrix based on the level of intensity and setting. The more thrilling and unique the idea, the further to the right it would be placed. At the same time, I would evaluate its setting. The further the idea was from city life and civilization, the higher the idea would be positioned on the matrix. Ultimately, the closer the idea was positioned to the convergence on the top right corner, the more on-brand it would be.

While working as the marketing director for Maverik, I was tasked to develop a name for a ridiculously large breakfast burrito stuffed with bacon, ham, sausage, potato, egg, and cheese. The name of the burrito would need to create interest and inform the customer that it was a really big breakfast burrito, while reinforcing the Maverik brand.

"Let's just call it what it is so our customers won't get confused— *The Maverik Extra-large Breakfast Burrito*," offered one employee.

Where on the Thrilling and Unique continuum would that name be placed? Where on the Adventurous Setting continuum would it be placed? That name was neither thrilling nor unique, and nothing about it suggested an adventurous setting. Best drop this into the lower left corner or into the trash.

"What if we called it the M.O.A.B., short for the "mother of all burritos?"

I placed this idea on the brand matrix. Moab is city in Utah and happened to be a mountain bike Mecca, which meant it rated high on the Adventurous Setting continuum. Using it to name a burrito would definitely be unexpected, and the "mother of all burritos" certainly sounded audacious, so it would rate high on the Thrilling and Unique scales. It looked like we had a winner!!

Creating a **brand matrix** is a fantastic method of radically reducing personal bias when evaluating ideas that will affect the strength of your brand.

Are you ready for launch!

At this point, you have defined the four critical elements of your **brand strategy**.
- F Found your **brand spark**
- I Identified your target customer(s). (Maybe a persona for each customer segment.)
- R Realized your **core belief**
- E Established your brand adjectives

If you went for extra credit, you even listed some aspirational brands, drafted a Desired Customer Reaction, or created a **brand matrix**. If so, I'm giving you an A+!

These important decisions in your **brand strategy** serve as the foundation of your brand and as a kind of lens to help you filter and focus decisions and ideas.

Before you begin building your website or designing your logo, the four elements of your **brand strategy** need to be evaluated as a whole to ensure that they both compliment and complement each other and are cohesive. You've heard the expression, "You can't see the forest for the trees"? It means you are unable to understand or see a situation clearly because you are too involved in it and are too fixated on minor details.

Unless you alter your perspective, you can get lost in the process.

The next step is testing the FIRE in your **brand strategy** to determine if you need to make any tweaks.

Review and Test

Reflection is one of the most underused yet powerful tools for success.

**– Richard Carlson Ph. D Author,
Don't Sweat the Small Stuff**

In 8th grade, I remember drawing an elf holding a sword prepared to do battle. (Dungeons and Dragons was a big deal in my childhood so don't judge.) I loosely sketched the overall figure and then leaned in close to work on the cool details of the face and head. After 30 minutes rendering eyes that looked wet and expressive, and finally getting the nose and mouth perfect, I leaned back to admire the whole composition certain it would be worthy of a college scholarship, but something wasn't quite right. The face looked awesome, but the head was way too large for the body. To make it look right, I had to either erase and redraw the totally awesome head or erase the body and re-sketch it to be in scale with the head. Even though a small portion of the drawing was fantastic, the whole drawing was terrible because all the pieces didn't fit together.

I learned my lesson early on that you need to keep changing your perspective and constantly evaluate the relationship of every element to ensure everything was in proportion before spending time on all the fun details.

To this point, you've been doing some really hard work brainstorming, evaluating, and making decisions with your **brand trust** to create a **brand strategy** to help you stay true and focused. Now would be a good time to get some fresh feedback from people who have not been involved in your brand development process before you create the design elements that will represent your brand to your customers.

 *Take Action*

STEP 1: Assemble Your Panel of Reason.

Assemble a **Panel of Reason** (not your **brand trust**) which should consist of mentors, potential customers, trusted friends and partners. These people should genuinely care about you and have your best interests in mind. Schedule a meeting with them for a couple of hours to review what you've developed and ask for constructive feedback.

One of my favorite places to meet is at a restaurant with a private dining room. It provides a new environment with fewer work distractions. It has the added benefit of readily available munchies and soft drinks so you can keep your panel energized.

Once your **Panel of Reason** is assembled, inform them that you are working on your company's brand and have selected each of them because you value their opinion. Let them know you want their honest feedback to make sure you are capturing the essence of your brand.

It's very easy for your panel to get side tracked. Ask them to hold on to their comments and questions until you've finished presenting so they can see how all of the pieces of the brand fit together. You are not seeking consensus, so you don't need them all to agree. You just need their perspective.

STEP 2: Present Your Brand Strategy

Begin your meeting by explaining that you would like to get their perspective on four principles of your brand's foundation: your **brand spark, target customer, core belief** and **brand description**. Then, briefly describe your product or service so everyone on your panel is on the same page.

Share your **brand spark** and how you found it. Explain why you feel it is authentic to your organization and unique in your industry.

Describe your target customer in detail. Describe their demographics and psychographics and explain how you came to that description. You may want to share your customer persona(s).

Articulate your **core belief.** Explain why it's important to your business and how you arrived at that definition.

Finally, list the adjectives you've selected to describe your brand. This would also be a good time to share your *Desired Customer Reaction* or **brand matrix** if you've developed one.

This presentation should take about 15 minutes.

STEP 3: Accept Feedback.

The next step is to ask for specific feedback. Your objective is to learn if the brand elements you've presented feel authentic to your business and fit together. Look for feedback that shows greater synergy between the FIRE elements.

Please do not ask, "Do you like it?" Remember, unless members of your panel are a sample of your target customer, it doesn't matter if it appeals to them. It's only important if it will appeal to your customers.

Use these questions to guide your discussion.

1. *"Do you think my brand spark is authentic to my business and unique in my industry?"*
2. *"Is the description of my target customer(s) on point?"* Your panel might be able to identify a customer segment you overlooked or add insight to the customer segments you've defined.
3. *"What do I need to emphasize or de-emphasize in my* brand spark *to better appeal to my target customer?"*
4. *"Do my personal actions represent my stated core belief?"*
5. *"How do you think my target customer(s) would respond to my core belief if I made it public?"*
6. *"Can you think of any of my competitors that use any of the adjectives I've listed to describe my brand?"*
7. *"Which adjectives should I emphasize in my brand? Am I missing any adjectives?"*
8. *"Do any of these ideas feel like they just don't fit?"*

Underscore any of your brand positions that were received with nodding heads and voices of affirmation. Ask follow-up questions and determine if you need to adjust any of your decisions that received furrowed brows and sour expressions. Write down specific comments and direction so you can present them to your **brand trust**.

At the conclusion of the meeting, thank the panel for their time and let them know you will take their feedback to heart.

Word of caution: I've been involved with a rebrand project where the initial branding foundational ideas were leaked to other employees in the company before we had an opportunity to review them as a whole. Inside information is a form of valuable corporate social currency, and it's common for employees to share that information with co-workers because it makes them feel important. The leaks came from employees that assumed the ideas we were discussing were decisions when, in reality, they were only ideas being considered and evaluated. Each of our meetings brought the executive team closer and closer to a clearer description of the brand, but each leak eroded confidence in the corporate leadership because employees interpreted evolutions to ideas as indecision. So, before releasing any employees in your **Panel of Reason** into their natural habitat, stress the importance of keeping conversations confidential to allow you time to prepare a strategy for rolling out the brand in a disciplined, well-planned process.

STEP 4: Review Feedback with your Brand Trust.

Now that you've received insights from your **Panel of Reason**, schedule a meeting with your **brand trust** to share the panel's feedback and evaluate their suggestions to determine which ideas, if any, ought to be incorporated into your **brand strategy**. Remember, your **Panel of Reason** provides insight to weigh against you and your teams' objectives and desires. Decide to make any revisions to your **brand strategy** while their input is still fresh on your mind.

If the feedback you receive from your **Panel of Reason** requires a complete do over, resist the urge to defend what you've done. Pause and breathe. Members of that panel will be composed of people who care about you and want you to be successful. So, take the time and effort to see your presentation from their perspective. Then measure their feedback against your heart. Their feedback may have saved you from failure. Starting this process anew at *Find your Brand Spark,* armed with their perspective, may set you on a far better course.

However, you are not obligated to do everything they tell you to do. You are the captain of your ship. If your original plan feels right, go for it! Your business is your baby and you'll second guess yourself forever if you don't do things the way you feel are right in your heart. You won't be the first successful business person to beat the odds by doing things your way.

Celebrate!

Congratulations! You have FIRE'd up your **brand strategy**! Use it as your guide in Part III to select building blocks of your brand that will reinforce your **brand personality** and help you stand out from your competitors.

Part III
The Building Blocks of Your Brand

"Make no small plans; they have no power to stir men's blood."

– *Daniel Burnham, Architect*

In Part II you made important decisions to define your **brand strategy**. In Part III you will use it to filter the selection of your brand's colors, patterns, textures, images, fonts, vocabulary, and sound. I'll shed light on their inherent personalities and meanings and guide you through the process of selecting the right ones to represent and reinforce your **brand strategy**. Then, I will show you how to use those brand elements to design a logo and develop a **Brand Bible** to represent your brand.

Establish Your Brand's Look and Feel

"Everything has a voice."
– **Dennis Snow**

By now, you're probably chomping at the bit to get some sales and marketing material produced because you've got a trade show or a big online launch coming up. Patience young Padawan learner, a Jedi of branding, soon you will be.

Your **brand strategy**, like the bottom 9/10ths of an iceberg, is invisible to your customers, but it's the base that supports what's visible on the surface. Your customers are exposed to websites, videos, podcasts, social media channels, pictures, radio commercials, billboards, packaging design, live events, store fronts, charities, and more. Each is crafted using visual and verbal brand elements like colors, textures, images, fonts/typography, tone, language, and vocabulary which have inherent personality characteristics associated with them.

This step is about curating elements of your visual and verbal language to convey the personality and emotional response you have established in your **brand strategy** in a way that grabs attention in an appealing and memorable way.

Colors

There are literally millions of colors to choose from so how do you pick the right one(s) for your brand? Do you choose a color that your competitors aren't using so you can stand out? Do you choose your favorite color?

Choose colors that reinforce the feeling or personality you want associated with your brand. The good news is that you don't have to guess which colors they are. You can use color psychology.

Color psychology is the study of hues as a determinant of human behavior and can be used intentionally to elicit specific emotions in your brand.

In their study, *Exciting Red and Competent Blue: The Importance of Color in Marketing,* Lauren I. Labrecque and George R. Milne concluded that "purchasing intent is greatly affected by colors due to the impact they have on how a brand is perceived. This means that colors influence how a consumer views the 'personality' of the brand in question…"[3]

The effect colors have on our emotions is influenced by cultures and personal experiences. For example, the color white is often associated with purity, simplicity, and innocence in Western culture but in Eastern cultures, white is symbolically linked to death and sadness.

While colors are not perceived exactly the same by all people in all cultures, it is generally accepted in the U.S. and other

---

[3] Lauren I. Labrecque and George R. Milne, "Exciting Red and Competent Blue: The importance of color in marketing." Journal of the Academy of Marketing Science, 2012

English-speaking countries that specific colors elicit a narrow range of emotions and associations.

For example: Red is associated with passion, energy, aggression. Yellow is associated with joy, happiness, cheerfulness, optimism. Light blue is the color most linked to creativity and sky blue is the most calming shade of blue and helps a person relax and feel safe and serene.

If the adjectives you selected to describe your brand in E-Establish Your Brand Adjectives are warm, sincere, mature, feminine and deeply emotional, you might choose colors like burgundy, dark purple, mahogany, or emerald green, which are associated with those descriptors.

If you described your brand as friendly, fun, youthful, bright, and happy, you'll choose yellows, oranges, true blues, and bright greens.

One of the easiest ways to select a color that is associated with an emotion is to search the internet. Simply search using the term "color associated with (insert emotion.)" I just searched "color associated with hunger" and discovered that yellow and orange are colors that make people feel hungry and, when combined with the color red (which is associated with energy and passion), creates passionate hunger. Just take a look at the logos for Wendy's, McDonald's, and In-n-Out as excellent examples. Imagine if their colors were dark pea-green and gray (emotions = neutral, dull, dirty, conservative, sophisticated, depression, jealousy, greed, sickness, cowardice, discord). For some reason, I've lost my appetite.

Great brands like Coca-Cola and McDonald's use their colors consistently on everything and would never approve of a color that was "close enough." They clearly communicate their color expectations in their **Brand Bible** (which we will address in the next chapter) and expect their vendors to get it right. They won't take delivery on anything that isn't the right color.

Here is a quick vocabulary lesson on color you can use to communicate with a designer or impress your friends.

> *Color is a generic term that applies to how our brains interpret light that is reflected off objects and surfaces into our eyes. It's also used to indicate a specific shade, hue or value of a color. Pure black, white, and the shades of gray in between are colorless, but for some reason we all still refer to them as a "color."*
>
> *Hue refers to the pure, fully saturated spectrum of colors. Think blue, purple, violet, red, orange, yellow, green and all the transitions between.*
>
> *Value refers to the relative darkness or lightness of a color. Think light blue or dark blue.*
>
> *Tinting is adding white to a color. You can lighten the value of a color by tinting.*
>
> *Shading is adding black to a color. You can darken the value of a color by shading.*
>
> *Tone is adding a shade of gray to a color which tends to remove saturation (desaturate) and visually soften the color.*
>
> *RGB is an abbreviation for Red, Green, and Blue used in producing colors on digital screens like TV's, monitors, phones and tablets. We see colors on those devices based on the amount of red, green, and blue light emitted through pixels. Varying amounts of power per color on a pixel can create millions of color variations. Some colors are so saturated and so bright that there is no ink that can adequately reproduce them. These colors are "out of gamut."*
>
> *CMYK is an abbreviation for Cyan, Magenta, Yellow, and Black and is used in color printing. It's also called "process printing" because variations in color are created using a process of the printer*

> laying down different sized inks droplets next to other ink droplets. Your desktop printer will have versions of these inks and when laying down various amounts of ink adjacent to other inks will yield a wide spectrum of printed color.
>
> *Spot Color* is a term used to define a specific color created using sophisticated pigments to produce subtle and precise color variations. These specific colors are referenced most commonly in the Pantone Matching System or PMS. Each color has a number associated with it.

 *Take Action*

STEP 1: Choose Your Colors.

Select a color that elicits the most important single adjective that describes your brand. Make sure that it isn't too similar to any of your competitors so that your brand remains distinct. So, if most of your competitors use blues in their advertising or packaging, avoid using the same blue hue or you run the risk of getting lost in the mix.

This is your "primary" color and will serve as the most prominent color in your logo and other brand elements. Next choose one secondary color for your brand that looks good with your primary color and will elicit other important emotions you've described in E-Establish Your Brand Adjectives. Finally, choose one or two colors as accent colors that look good with your primary and secondary colors.

STEP 2: Putting Your Colors to Use

Use your primary color on nearly everything created, promotion-wise, religiously, as if it were a branding commandment. This doesn't mean that you have to flood every wall and every page with your primary color, but make sure your customers can't miss it. And be consistent. It needs to be the identical color.

If your business is going to be doing a lot of commercial printing for packaging or sales brochures, take printed samples of your colors (magazines, packaging, or your desktop printer) to a local printer. Your printer can show you a PMS (Pantone Matching System) color swatch book. The Pantone color system is a standard that all professional printers use to ensure they print colors the same, regardless of the printing equipment they use. With the printing professional's help, select the closest process and spot colors that match your printed samples. Make a note of the CMYK color mix (percentage of Cyan, Magenta, Yellow, and Black inks) and spot color number for each of your primary and secondary colors. Then write them down. You'll need to refer to them when you develop your **Brand Bible** in Part IV.

Write down your colors and/or tape swatches of your colors in the *Ignite Your Brand* workbook for quick and easy reference.

Now that you've selected the colors that will help you stand out from the crowd and elicit the emotional response you want from your target customers, it's time for you to consider some patterns and textures to visually reinforce the look and feel of your brand.

Imagery & Pictures

Images in the form of photographs, illustrations, and videos are powerful ways to communicate your **brand personality** because they tell a story in an instant and are extremely easy to recall.

If you think about your favorite brands, you'll likely be able to quickly recall an ad, video, or social media post because they use images to tell their story that are easy to remember. Take Tony the Tiger. When you see an image of him you are more likely to think of a box of Kellogg's Frosted Flakes, or of milk being poured over cereal, than if you were to read a list of ingredients or peruse the nutritional information. It's because the human brain has the ability to process images 60,000-times more quickly than verbal or written information. It's called the Picture Superiority Effect.[4]

Images are composed of two elements: the subject matter, and style. Both subject matter and style can express an emotion or personality.

Subject matter is the focus or object in your image. It can be your products. It can be characters like Tony the Tiger, celebrities like Taylor Swift, spokespeople like Progressive's Flo, or a specific customer persona like Pabst Blue Ribbons' blue-collar "everyman." The subject matter is the physical thing your picture, video, or illustration is focusing on.

Style is how the subject looks and feels in an illustration, photograph, video, or product design. It is affected by lighting and exposure in images taken with a camera. It is influenced by the tools an artist uses to create an illustration. Style can also be expressed through composition and editing. For example, Red Bull uses wobbly-lined illustrations and animations for its "Red Bull gives you wings" print and TV campaigns. TAG Heuer uses a style of desaturated photography of famous people wearing its watches with simplified backgrounds and strong lighting in its ads. Dove celebrates real beauty by featuring photographs of real women that

---

[4] Curran, T.; Doyle, J., "Picture superiority doubly dissociates the ERP correlates of recollection and familiarity." Journal of Cognitive Neuroscience. 23 (5): 1247–1262. doi:10.1162/jocn.2010.21464. PMID 20350169. (2011).

haven't been photo retouched on white backgrounds. The Corona beer brand frequently places its bottles of beer in the setting of a white sandy beach with blue skies accented with palm trees because it wants its product to elicit relaxed feelings associated with beachside vacations. While researching Corona beer ads I discovered the same beach photo in the background was used in many of its other ads. Talk about consistency!!!

Many years ago, I worked with an ad agency on a campaign for its credit union client. The credit union wanted to increase the number of small business loans in its portfolio. Banks and credit unions typically use conservative images to convey serious professionalism. Our research revealed that the competition was using photographs and videos of attractive individuals posing successfully in front of their small businesses. Our client wanted to represent that same level of trustworthiness but also wanted to describe its brand as friendly and approachable. We knew that if we tried to create a different message using the same type of conservative images our message would get lost in the sea of sameness.

To get our message to penetrate the minds and hearts of our potential customers we first needed to get their attention. We had to do something different. Radically different. We devised an idea to tell stories of fun cartoon characters building whimsical businesses. One of the characters started a business called Guaca-Chip Cookies where cookies were made with avocados, and

another character started a French fry and baked potato restaurant called Spudtopia.

The style of illustration and the yellow backgrounds we used in its ads were designed to stand apart from the competition, be easy to recall, and help their potential customers feel that the brand was friendly and approachable. As a result, the ads got attention and its small business loan portfolio grew by more than 300%.

If your brand can be described as simple, easy, fun, light, or something similar, illustration and animation is a fitting style.

Chick-fil-A employs realistic-looking Holstein cows holding paint brushes or A-frame signs on white backgrounds. These boycotting bovines paint their own picket signs and ask us to join their righteous fight against burger consumption by encouraging us to eat delicious chicken sandwiches. These whimsical black and white images paint a strong contrast to the typical images fast food restaurants use and have proven to be highly recognizable and memorable.

As you can see, there are all kinds of ways to use images to strengthen and reinforce your **brand personality**. The key to selecting or creating the right kind of image is to make sure it helps convey the attitude and personality of your brand.

So, what will be the subject of your marketing and advertising?

Take Action

STEP 1: Brainstorm Your Subject Matter

Brainstorm subjects that will get attention and represent the benefit of your product or service. If your product helps people save time, depict a scene that inspires a great way to spend the time they saved. If your product helps people lose weight, show off the results.

Do you have a product that has a unique design feature that would be recognizable in a photograph? Is there a celebrity that exemplifies your company's personality and values? Can you create a virtual character or spokesperson like the Aflac Duck, the Geico Gecko, or the Dos Equis' most interesting man in the world to express your company's personality?

Does your company need to simplify complex ideas for your target customer? If so, you may want to choose a friendly actor who can deliver clear, relaxed messages. You can also have illustrations or animations created to explain what your products or services do.

Write down the subjects you've brainstormed.

STEP 2: Source Your Images

You can get your images from two great sources– online stock libraries, or commissioned illustrators and photographers.

Stock image websites are online galleries where professional illustrators and photographers sell their images for commercial use. It's one of the most accessible and most affordable resources. Jump on a web browser and search using the keyword "stock images" and you'll see a long list of sites to choose from. I've personally used iStock, 123RF, and Shutterstock with amazing results. Cost for a single image can be as low as a few dollars. They all have robust search fields, so type in the subject you are looking for, such as: laughing kids, happy flowers, angry moms, or whatever, and browse the results until you find some images that evoke the emotions you want associated with your brand.

If you want a custom illustration or photograph, you'll want to collect some inspirational references for the illustrator or the photographer. Collect five or six images on the internet that have the look and feel of what you want for your brand.

Then, give those references along with a photo or description of your subject matter, to your favorite photographer or illustrator. You can hop on a website like societyillustrators.org, fiverr.com, freelancer.com, or 99designs.com and browse their talent until you find an illustrator or photographer with a portfolio that matches the look and feel you're searching for. I've had tremendous success with talent from freelancer.com and they can be very affordable.

When you curate a library of images with a specific look and feel and use them consistently in your marketing and advertising, they help you stand out and to be recognized, creating a strong emotional connection to your customer.

Write a description of the type of images you think will best convey your brand and message in your *Ignite Your Brand* workbook.

Patterns, Textures, and Materials

Patterns, textures, and materials convey powerful emotions and help place your brand in a specific emotional setting. When we see patterns, textures, and materials in branded marketing elements, our minds can subconsciously draw an emotional association to the experience we've had with that texture and connect it to the brand that uses that texture in their branding. For example, if you see rough pinewood bark, you might think of a mountain forest with associated feelings of being outdoors, camping, or hiking. If you see polka dots, you may associate them with retro-fashioned polka-dot dresses and bikinis. Blue denim could be associated with 50's popular rebel fashion or rugged, old-fashioned miners and farmers. Textures help us recall feelings based on experiences.

Imagine amber liquid pouring into a small, thick glass sitting on a plank of dark scratched wood. What is being poured? Is it apple juice or whisky? We've seen that same wood countertop in western movies and TV commercials where the barkeep pours whisky or tequila into a shot glass. A varnished, distressed wood *texture* would be a great texture to use if you were building a brand for Jack Daniels.

Louis Vuitton created its own pattern that it uses relentlessly in advertising and product design. The pattern consists of its LV initials and simple flower shapes in gold on a field of brown. Gold represents wealth, affluence, prestige. Brown is a warm, rich color that complements gold and is associated with strength and security. The pattern is so distinct and used so consistently that women can spot a Louis Vuitton bag by simply getting a glimpse of the pattern.

 *Take Action*

STEP 1: Select Your Textures.

Find or create textures that exude the feeling you want in your brand and incorporate them consistently in your marketing and advertising materials the way you would your logo or type style.

Here is a list of textures to jump-start your thought processes:
- White Sand- peaceful beach. Great for a relaxed coastal theme business.
- Aged Parchment- old, antique, historic, vintage, European
- Cold Pressed Steel- industrial, gritty, strong, cool
- Smooth planed light wood- natural, ecological, comfortable, friendly
- Black Leather- American, tough, rebellious
- Polished Aluminum or Stainless Steel- technical, professional, clean, clinical, sterile
- Diamond Plating- edgy, automotive, tough
- Closeup of Jungle Leaves- fresh, tropical, alive

- White Linen- expensive, sophisticated, proper
- Cold-pressed Watercolor Paper- clean, elegant, expensive, handcrafted, natural
- Dark Dirt- natural, organic, environmental
- Blue Sky- light, airy, environmentally friendly, happy, calm

STEP 2: Research The Competition.

Conduct your own competitive research to make sure the textures you choose are not being used by competitors in your market. Too many beach-front real estate companies use textures of sandy beaches and images of palm trees in their brand, so give yourself creative liberty and select textures that your competitors don't use or, as I will repeat, time and time again, you'll risk getting lost in the mix.

STEP 3: Use Your Texture Wisely.

Use your textures the same way you would use cologne or perfume; enough to make an impression but not too much to overpower everything else. For example: If my business made whisky and selected an old thick plank of wood as a brand texture, I would use it as the surface on which all of my products were photographed. I might use it behind the logo on one side of my business cards, the front, or back cover of a sales brochure. However, I wouldn't use it on every page and on every background and on every wall. That's too much of a good thing, that's overkill! Like the time I ate too many Hershey's Mr. Goodbars. It didn't end well...

There are limitless options you can choose from, so be creative. When you select unique textures that reinforce your company personality and use them religiously, you'll genuinely and memorably stand out.

Write a description of the textures you want to use for your brand in your *Ignite Your Brand* workbook.

Typography

Font design has been around since humans first began to scrawl. Fonts are strongly associated with time, place, and emotion. They help you tell your story and are a great design tool to help you stand out from your competitors. Consistently using specific fonts also helps you organize the hierarchy of your message so your audience can more easily digest it.

How are you?
How are you?
How are you?
How are you?
How are you?
HOW ARE YOU?
HOW ARE YOU?
How are you?
How are you?

Master of Visual Social Media, Louise Myers, provides a perfect explanation of personalities associated with fonts.

"Fonts are classified into five broad categories.

1. Serif typefaces have little feet or wings at each end. Serif fonts are seen as traditional, stable, practical, serious, mature, formal, scholarly, corporate, and business-like.

2. Slab Serif is a certain kind of serif typeface that has thick, squared-off serifs. Slab Serif fonts are more modern, but can also be perceived as bold, harsh, rude, assertive, coarse, or masculine.

3. Sans Serif fonts are typefaces without feet, which makes them look clean and understated. Their personality is contemporary, sometimes sleek, and often elegant.

4. Script typefaces look like handwriting or calligraphy. They can range from casual to formal. They have soft, organic, and humanistic qualities that give them a warm personality.

5. Display typefaces have the most diverse and outspoken personalities. Their character forms often suggest a personality from a specific genre, era, or period of time."[5]

---

[5] Louise Myers, "Font Personality: How to Choose Your Best" Visual Social

One of my favorite uses of branded type is from Chick-fil-A. The font they use looks like it was painted by cows. Their font helps tell the story of their brand.

If your brand is rugged and western oriented, you will use fonts from that era that have rough, distressed edges. If your brand is elegant and sophisticated, you may want to select thin calligraphic type fonts. If your brand is contemporary, you may want to choose a sans serif font. If your brand is loud, use a thicker, heavier type of font. If your brand is quiet, reserved, or understated, use fonts that are more lightweight, yet still impactful in appearance.

Typically, your brand will have a headline font, an accent font, and a body copy font.

Example for a fun, lighthearted brand.	Example for a modern, contemporary brand.
HEADLINES	**HEADLINES**
Accent	*Accent*
Copy and Text	Copy and Text

The headline font is a typestyle that exudes your **brand personality**. It is often the same, or a variation of, the font you use in your logo. Use your headline font for headlines and titles and anywhere you want to draw considerable attention.

Your accent font is not as loud and should be easier to read at a smaller size than your headline font. Use the accent font for chapter headings or where you need to emphasize an idea, call to action, or tagline. It should complement the personality of your brand.

Your body copy is the type style you will use the most. It should convey a tiny hint of the personality of your brand and be easy to read. Use it for anything you write in a paragraph such as advertising copy, internal forms, and sales letters.

One of the best tools for finding fonts is, once again, the internet. Just use the search keyword "fonts." Most online font libraries are organized by descriptors, so try finding fonts using descriptors that are similar to the adjectives you've selected to describe your brand. You can often type in a few words to see how the fonts look using different words. There are literally thousands of fonts to choose from and many are free. Look for font families that have subtle variations of fonts that can be used for headline, accent, and body copy.

Your fonts are an essential element of your **brand personality**. Make it a requirement to use your designated fonts for everything including, especially, internal communications such as HR documents, memos, presentations, etc. The brand standards you hold employees to at the corporate level set an expectation for the whole business.

 *Take Action*

FIND YOUR FONTS

Search a font library on the internet or also in your favorite word processing application on your computer and find a headline font, accent font, and body copy font that represents the personality of your brand. Write down the name of those fonts in your *Ignite Your Brand* workbook for quick and easy reference.

Vocabulary

"G'day mate!"
"'Sup holmes?"
"Howdy y'all!"
"Learn, you must."

Each of these short phrases immediately gives you a feeling of tone and personality because each has been used within specific contexts you are familiar with. The verbal language provides opportunities for your business to stand out by weaving words and phrases into your communication that are strongly associated with the personality of your brand.

I was asked to help re-brand an auto dealership franchise in the great state of Wyoming and I discovered their brand had a very independent, non-conformist spirit with a very unique sense of humor. My clients knew they needed to adopt a remarkable brand to stand out from the unremarkable sameness common to all the other dealerships, so the president of the company made a bold move and proposed to call the franchise *Rocky Mountain Yeti*. My knee jerk reaction was to encourage them not to, but I surprised myself when I said, "Well, that's different. Let's all think about it tonight and touch base tomorrow morning."

All afternoon and late into the night, my imagination was sparked with marketing ideas, slogans, advertisements, and promotions on the mythical Yeti theme, and when we all met on a phone conference call the following morning, I was happy to discover that we all had similar brainstorms. The Yeti character became their **brand spark** which inspired a handful of phrases and words that they use in their messaging to convey their values and personality.

"Legendary service," wild, untamed, discover, mythical, "Boring Sucks."

Here is how they were used: "Discover used car deals that are legendary!" "At Rocky Mountain Yeti, legendary service is not a myth." "We stand behind every car we sell with our legendary powertrain warranty."

How do I incorporate this vocabulary process into my own marketing materials? Let me use my own business as an example.

My branding consulting business is called Ernburn (a nickname my twin brother gave me as kid), and I created a logo of a flaming e to help potential customers remember me. I've chosen to develop a vocabulary on the *burn* theme. I try to use words like *spark, ignite, kindle, flame, smoke, heat, light,* and *start* in my messaging.

 *Take Action*

STEP 1- Brainstorm Your Branded Vocabulary

Spend a few minutes brainstorming words that you can use to reinforce your brand.

STEP 2- Say It Straight

Next, write an advertising or marketing message as clearly and as plainly as you can in two or three sentences. My first draft for a one-sentence introduction read, "I help companies develop strong brands."

STEP 3- Say It Great

Then look for words in your message that you can replace with *your* vocabulary words. My introduction became, "I help companies *ignite remarkable* brands." This sentence has been crafted to reinforce my brand by drawing a connection to Ernburn using my brand vocabulary.

When you've curated your vocabulary and phrases, sprinkle them subtly into your messaging like fine black truffle oil. A little goes a long way.

Write the words you want associated with your brand in your workbook.

Audio- The sound of your brand

Music and the human voice are powerful devices for your brand toolbox and never in history has it been easier and less expensive to communicate using audio/visual tools. To compete in today's world, it will be important for you to develop a signature sound for your brand. There are two elements for your audio brand: voice and music.

Voice

Once again, it's time to refer to the descriptors you established in E- Establish Your Brand Adjectives because voices and music have natural associations to personality in the same way colors, fonts, textures, and images do.

If your brand was described as intense, solid, and authoritative, a voice similar to James Earl Jones would be fitting. If your brand was described as western, rustic, and tough like Coors beer or Ram trucks, you might settle on a voice like Sam Elliot's. And if your brand was perky, friendly and intelligent, you might pick a voice like Katie Couric's.

I've used famous celebrities as examples, but if you don't have a large budget, you can use some fantastic online voiceover services such as voicetalentnow.com and voice123.com. Each website has a large roster of talent. Find the best match for your brand by filtering talent using words similar to the descriptor words you selected in E- Establish Your Brand Adjectives. (I told you they were important!) You can even listen to samples of their vocal performances.

Most online voice services can turn around your project within 24 hours and provide more than one performance of your script so you can choose the one that fits your brand best. It's a lot of fun, very affordable, and extremely easy to hire voice talent.

 *Take Action*

Step 1: Write a script.

Do your best to write out a script that captures your target customers' attention, highlights the primary customer benefit(s) and concludes with a call to action. If you find yourself struggling to write one, you can hire a writer. I suggest you ask your employees, friends, coworkers and social network if they know anyone with writing skills. You may have a great writer in your own back yard!

If your audio file has time constraints like a radio ad that allows for 15-, 30-, and 60-second ads, read it out loud to get a sense of timing and rewrite it until you can comfortably read it within your allotted time frame. Work on an average 150 words per minute of spoken audio for your script.

Step 2: Record a scratch track.

Record your own performance of the script and upload it along with the script so the talent can hear your local pronunciation of industry words and where you want emphasis placed.

Step 3: Select your voice talent.

Listen to the performance reels of the talent you are considering. When you find a great performance that matches your brand, send that person a request to perform your script along with any time constraints. Great voice actors have a broad range of characters and voices they perform so I've found it very helpful to reference the specific performance from their sample reel that caught your attention.

Write a description of your voice talent in the back of your workbook for easy reference. You may also want to write in the name of the voice artist so you can find them again.

If the first audio promotion connects with your target market, try to use the same voice talent for future audio work to increase your customers' ability to recognize your brand when they hear it.

Music

"Music moves people. It connects people in ways that no other medium can."
  – Macklemore

If you're developing a podcast, video series, radio commercial, TV commercial, tradeshow, YouTube channel, or any other audio/video content, you're going to need music that reinforces your **brand personality**.

Music is as old as the human race. It is a universal language. Certain instruments, rhythms, harmonies, and tempos provoke an immediate emotional response and connect with different kinds of personalities.

If your brand is intimate, natural, friendly, and upbeat, you might select music that features an acoustic guitar, whistling, or maybe even a bongo drum.

If your brand is sophisticated, powerful, and bold, you might choose symphonic sounding music that can be recorded using a symphony orchestra, or synthesized by a professional digital musician if you're on a smaller budget.

Knowing how to describe your brand's personality makes it easier to select the type of music you should use to reinforce it.

Collen Fahey, the U.S. Managing Director of Sixiéme Son, a global leader in audio branding, explained: "At its core, music is language – when used well, it can convey meaning with great clarity. To get started with audio branding, it's essential to first clarify what our brand stands for and then evaluate the sounds that might help translate those values into the language of music." [6]

Music also helps people recall information. According to David C. Rubin, a specialist in autobiographical memory and oral traditions, music helps people remember. This is extremely valuable information, especially when you want someone to remember your brand.

Although nerdy, the following bit of science in an article from BBC Culture and written by Tiffany Jenkins is extremely helpful in understanding how sounds can quickly and subconsciously unlock associations with your brand.

"The hippocampus and the frontal cortex are two large areas in the brain associated with memory and they take in a great deal of information every minute. Retrieving it is not always easy. It doesn't simply come when you ask it to. Music helps because it provides a rhythm and rhyme and sometimes alliteration which helps to unlock that information with cues. It is the structure of the song that helps us to remember it, as well as the melody and the images the words provoke."[7]

So, if you've already defined the personality of your brand and have selected descriptive words as reference, how do you convert

---

[6] Colleen Fahey, "How Audio Enhances, Your Brand Content: Find Your Signature Sound" Content Market Institute, November 8, 2013
[7] Tiffany Jenkins, "Why does music evoke memories?" BBC Culture, Oct 21, 2014

that information into music you can use? It's much easier now than just a couple decades ago.

I remember the days when I had to book time with a music composer in a really cool (expensive) sound studio with lots of technical (expensive) gear to develop a music background for a project. Did I mention it was expensive? And it took a lot of time.

However, thanks to today's far more affordable equipment prices, a wider pool of talent has access to professional quality digital audio tools. Getting your ears on high-quality music has become more convenient and more affordable than ever.

Hundreds of artists create music to suit every mood, genre, and key for every purpose. They post them online on stock music websites like soundstripe.com, stockmusic.net, and premiumbeat.com. Stock music means that it's pre-produced and ready for use. On stock music websites, you can search for music based on a wide variety of filters such as mood, characteristic, genre, energy, instrument, key, vocals, duration, and beats per minute/tempo. The advantages of using stock music is that it's instantly accessible and inexpensive, though a disadvantage of stock music is that the music you choose may also be used by your competitor, or another familiar product/brand.

 *Take Action*

OPTION #1 Big Budget

If you have the budget, share your **brand strategy** with a composer or commercial recording producer to work their magic on a highly customized and highly personal sound for your brand.

OPTION #2 On The Cheap

If you're trying to keep expenses low, use the online resources I've mentioned above. Simply log on and search for music using filter terms similar to the descriptors you've selected for your brand.

Think of your music as your audible logo and use it on all of your audio projects. The more you use it, the more your customers will associate it with your brand.

Summary

When you select **brand attributes** like fonts, images, colors, textures, vocabulary, and sound based on their inherent personality and use them consistently across all communication touch points, they will be singing from the same song book. Each voice will add strength and clarity to the others and will create a dynamic, strong harmony for your brand that's impossible to ignore and easy to recognize!

The brand elements you just finished curating, guided by your **brand strategy**, will be the key components in your logo, tagline, and **Brand Bible** masterpiece. Let's see how the pieces fit.

PART IV
Assembling the Parts

So, let it be written, so let it be done!"

– Yul Brynner- Ramses

You've written out a detailed brand foundation that describes your brand's look, feel, and personality and if you are as impatient as me, you're screaming, "Let's make something happen already!"

This chapter will explain how to use your **brand strategy** as a **brand lens** to focus the production of real-world marketing and communications materials such as your logo, tagline, and **Brand Bible**.

Design Your Logo

Logos are the graphic extension of the internal realities of a company.

– Saul Bass - graphic designer and Oscar- winning filmmaker

Every company should have an awesome logo. It should be so cool that your employees would be proud to wear it on their chest and your customers would want to buy your brands t-shirt, hoodie, or hat. Your logo is shorthand for your brand and should prompt the emotions you've previously defined to describe it. It often takes the form of a typeset name of your company and is frequently embellished by an image or icon that makes it unique and memorable.

Directly and indirectly (subliminally), your customers are bombarded with thousands of non-stop marketing messages every day. It's no wonder we all try to avoid advertisements by instead watching paid media subscriptions like Netflix, Hulu, Pandora, etc... This aversion to advertising is why your logo should be attractive to your customers and easy to identify, while prompting a mental connection to what your company does or sells.

Your logo will often be the first impression made on your customer and will follow you around like a tattoo, so take the advice of a guy who has created over a hundred logos– make it as impressive and impactful as you can with the budget you've got.

Logo design can vary in price. A good independent designer with over 10 years' experience may charge between $2,500-$7,500 for a well-designed logo. You can get less experienced designers to design a logo for you for about $500 or you can hire an agency that may charge tens of thousands.

If you're a small business owner or a startup on a budget, I recommend you use companies like logotournament.com, fiverr.com, logomatics.com, and Freelancer.com which usually provide you with dozens of options for a single low price. Freelancer.com has an option to post a 'contest' where you provide the requirements for your logo, offer a 'prize' based on your budget, and you can get up to 50 designs, but you only need give the prize to the one you like best. You can start for as little as $100.00. My favorite is logotournament.com because the user interface is intuitive, and I've received great results spending between $350 and $750 for a logo. I usually get over 100 logo submissions on every contest. (The more you pay, the better designers you'll attract and the more options you'll get to choose from.)

Regardless of whether you choose an online service, local designer, or design firm, they will want the information you've established in Part II when you sparked the FIRE in your brand. They will also need the building blocks of your brand that define your brand's visual and verbal language you established in Part III. If you're working with an online resource like logotournament.com, you can provide that information in their easy-to-follow, step-by-step project setup. If you're working with a local designer, you can simply share what you've developed thus far. They will also be super-impressed!

The more colors your logo has, the more expensive it will be to reproduce on SWAG items such as t-shirts, golf balls, embroidery, etc., so be sure to get the following versions of your logo:
- Full-color logo for digital printing and websites, videos, and other digital screens.
- Spot-color logo using only the brand colors you identified in Step 6.
- Single-color versions of your logo in black, white, and one in each of your primary, secondary and accent colors.

Here are four things to consider when developing a great logo.
1. Great logos allude to the type of product or service your company provides because it quickens the mental connection of your name to your offering. Try to incorporate some symbol or illustration that shows the customer the kind of business you are in.
2. You want your logo to be as simple as possible and easy to read in any size. Business cards used to be a big deal, but now your logo needs to be legible as a 16x16 pixel favicon in your web browser. Does it look good and is it easy to

read in black and white? Could you easily cut it out of vinyl and stick it on the back window of your car or truck? Lots of little details in your logo make it more complex and harder to read at smaller sizes.
3. Make sure it has appeal. It's true that beauty is in the eye of the beholder but look through the eyes of your target customers. A well-designed logo should be highly attractive to your target customers and elicit a positive emotional response. Validate your intuition by asking your best customers to review the logo options you are considering. If your mom says she hates it, thank her for her opinion and ignore it unless she is part of your target audience.
4. Make sure it pops. It needs to be distinguished from your competitors' logos using shape, color, and design. A well-designed logo should stand out like a bright-pink-and-yellow Easter egg in a cow pasture littered with cow patties. (Yes, I purposely inferred that many logos have cow patty appeal.)

This logo for the Spartan Golf Club is an excellent example because it alludes to the sport of golf through the use of a graphic illustration that is simultaneously a golfer and a Spartan's helmet, which quickens the mental connection to the company name. Even without the words "golf club" at the bottom, there is no question that this business is associated with golf and a Spartan. The duality of the illustration and its simplicity gives the logo natural appeal and helps it pop.

It's also illustrated using only one color (black) which means it's less expensive to print, cut out of vinyl for stickers, engrave on solid material for signs, and embroider on apparel. It's a hole in one!

The most important attribute of your logo is that *you* love it, because you're going to put it on everything and see it everywhere. Your logo will develop meaning to your customers the more they see it associated with what your business does.

Once you have your true-love logo, be sure to submit it for trademark. Trademarking protects your organization from companies who would purposely copy your logo or company name, or use one very similar to it, that could confuse your customers. It also protects your company from unknowingly infringing on someone else's existing logo as you won't be awarded a trademark if you have inadvertently created something similar to another company's logo.

You can do it yourself in about 90 minutes through the United States Patent and Trademark Office at uspto.org. You'll be charged an initial application fee for electronic filing which, at the time of writing, is between $225 and $275. You can also hire an attorney who can do all the paperwork for you for a couple of hundred dollars. (Personally, I think attorneys are worth it.)

You should also do this for the super-clever tagline you'll develop next.

Develop a Snappy Tagline

Too often, people focus on the "content" of the message rather than on the "memorability" of the slogan. Without memorability, a slogan is unlikely to accomplish much.

– Laura Ries - President of Ries & Ries

A tagline is a catch phrase or slogan frequently used in advertising messages to improve mental stickiness. Great taglines are easy to recall and help audiences connect a feeling to the benefit associated with a product or service. "Think Different." "Melts in your mouth not in your hands." "Got milk?" "Open Happiness."

Try one or both of the following techniques for developing your tagline, then write your tagline in your workbook.

TECHNIQUE #1 Product Feature – Customer Benefit

One of the best techniques is to write out what your customer does with the product and how that then benefits the customer. Then take that phrase and simplify it until only the heart and meaning remains.

One of my favorite taglines that uses this technique is Coca Cola's "Open Happiness." This may have started with, "When people open a bottle of Coca Cola, they feel happy." This was then condensed, several times, until it couldn't be condensed any further, yet the final result is by far the most effective.

Many years ago, my creative team developed a tagline for utahcars.com, a car dealership that sold cars exclusively online. We noted that buying cars at a dealership, for many, was an unhappy experience and shoppers often felt swindled or cheated in the process. The utahcars.com website promised complete transparency so buyers could make informed purchase decisions. As a result, customers could drive away feeling good about the amount of money they paid while avoiding the dreaded dealership experience.

My team brainstormed a list of taglines that followed the theme of making informed buying decisions and the good feeling that resulted.

Buy informed. Feel good.
Shop easy, be happy.
Buy cars the smart way and drive away happy.
Buy smart, drive happy.

Ultimately, we chose, "Buy smart, drive happy!" because "buy smart" suggested that smart people bought cars on utahcars.com and "drive happy" helped remind people that this new online company was in the automobile business and the customer benefit was happiness.

 *Take Action*

Write a short sentence describing how your product or service benefits your customer. Don't embellish. Just say it in as few words as possible. You may try writing it on a whiteboard or piece of paper. Then do your best to condense the message into as few words as possible.

TECHNIQUE #2 Customer Sentiment

What might customers say about your product or service? What might a customer say about your product that rings true? If your product or service is already available, ask members of your sales team the phrases they most often hear from their customers.

Is your product durable and tough like Timex watches? "Takes a licking and keeps on ticking." Energizer batteries keep their power for a long time and "Keep going and going…" M&M's candies "Melt in your mouth, not in your hands."

 *Take Action*

Write an ideal phrase that one or more of your customers might use to describe your product.

TECHNIQUE #3 Desired Customer Benefit

Brainstorm some short phrases that you would like your customers to say or think about you.

I've been to Disneyland many times and have witnessed pouting children arguing with frustrated, overheated parents but that didn't stop Disneyland from developing a tagline: "The Happiest Place on Earth!" Their tagline is what Disneyland *wants* their customers to think about them.

 *Take Action*

Write a short phrase that you'd like your customers to say about your business. This kind of tagline is more than marketing. It inspires and changes the way your employees approach their work in the company.

When it comes to writing a tagline French poet, writer, aristocrat, and aviator, Antoine de Saint-Exupery says it best, "Perfection is achieved, not when there is nothing more to add, but when there is nothing left to take away."

You'll know you've landed on a great tagline when it is short, sweet, and ignites you with creative advertising ideas.

Develop a Brand Bible (aka Brand Design Style Guide)

Give me six hours to chop down a tree and I will spend the first four sharpening the ax.

– Abraham Lincoln

To promote your amazing products or services, you'll need to produce packaging, brochures, websites, apps, sales presentations, and more. These branding touchpoints make impressions like flakes of snow that accumulate until becoming a noticeable avalanche of persuasiveness over time. Your brand touchpoints need to look and feel the same to make the cumulative effect work for you. And that's where your **Brand Bible** comes in.

A **Brand Bible** is a multi-page document that provides visual examples and clear instructions for producing sales and marketing materials in line with your brand that you, or any third party can reference. It is a visible manifesto for your brand. It affirms the personality of your company, who it serves, and how it serves them in the form of an easy-to-send-and-view document.

This document is called a **Brand Bible** because it's the final word on the brand, so breaking any of the brand commandments will bring upon you the judgments of the almighty Director of Marketing. (Very similar to a lake of fire and brimstone.) Do you think the Director of Marketing at Nike will turn a blind eye to a squished swoosh? Nay! Great brands don't compromise on the guidelines outlined in their Brand Bible.

Your Brand Bible should follow this outline:
- Company Introduction
- Brand Foundation
- Brand Spark
- Target Customer
- Core Belief
- Brand Description
- Design Elements
- Chosen Colors
- Textures and Patterns
- Materials
- Images
- Typography
- Vocabulary
- Logo Usage Guidelines
- Tagline
- Examples

Designers with sweet skills use graphic design programs like Adobe Illustrator or InDesign, but if you're not familiar with those programs don't sweat it. You can create your own Brand Bible in a program like Microsoft Word, or Apple Pages, Keynote or PowerPoint.

If you want to see examples of brand bibles using my process go to http://www.ernburn.com/kindling

If you want to be inspired by a huge variety of brand bibles go to www.canva.com.

 *Take Action*

Follow this outline to create your **Brand Bible** using the fonts, colors, textures, images, vocabulary, and tone you've established in Part III, Establish Your Brand's Looks and Feel.

First of all, design your cover page.

Put your logo and tagline on the front cover along with one of your selected textures, colors, or images as a background, border, or framing element.

Section 1- Your Brand Foundation

Page 1- Brand Spark. Using your headline font write down something like: "What makes (insert company name) different?" Then write out the description of your **brand spark** using your accent font. (You may want to accent this page with an image that reinforces what makes your business unique. Perhaps a photo of your building, product, logo, customer, founder, or a picture that represents how your business benefits your customer.)

Page 2- Core Customer. Using your headline font write: "Our Core Customer." Then write down a description of your core customer using your accent and body copy font. Include a photo to represent your customer in the photography style you selected in Part III. You might also want to create a customer avatar profile for each of your major customers from I-Identify Your Core Customer.

Page 3 Core Belief. Using your headline font write: "Our Core Belief." Then write down the **core belief** you defined in R-Realize Your Core Belief in your accent font. Add an image or a design element that helps reinforce your core belief.

Follow the same process above using headline fonts, images, accent fonts and body font to design pages for your **brand description** from E- Establish Your Brand Adjectives which could include one or more of the following:
1. **Aspirational Brands**- Place each brand logo next to a short paragraph that explains what you like about that brand that you hope to inspire in yours.
2. **Personality** or **Voice**- List the adjectives that describe your brand along with short definitions. This is sometimes called your "voice." It would be ideal if you can include a small icon, illustration, or image in the look and feel of your brand that represents each adjective.
3. **Desired Customer Reaction**- Write out your desired customer reaction in your accent font.
4. **Brand Matrix**- Create an image of your **brand matrix** using your company's fonts, colors and textures and place it on the page with a short paragraph that describes how to use it when evaluating marketing options.

Section 2- Design Elements (from Part III- Establishing Your Brands Look and Feel)

Colors- Create a headline called "Colors" in your headline font. Create shapes and fill them with your colors. Under each shape label each color: Primary Color, Secondary Color, or Accent Color in your accent font. Next to each color, write a short description in your body copy font that describes the emotional or psychological significance behind each color. (To make this page more interesting you may want to use color shapes from an element of your logo, or maybe an icon for each color that reinforces its significance.)

Textures and Patterns- Create a headline called "Textures and Patterns" in your headline font. Then place shapes filled with your textures or patterns next to a short description of when and where you would like them to be used. Are they going to be used as backgrounds for headers, footers, sidebars, etc.?

Materials- Place pictures or swatches for the kinds of surfaces you want used in your interior and exterior design.

Images- Create a headline called "Images" in your headline font. Place examples of the type of photos or illustrations you want to use along with a clear description of what makes them 'on-brand'. (If your brand is likely to make use of customer-generated photos or photography from a variety of sources, you may want to include examples of photos that are not in line with the brand and a clear explanation why. For example: photos with bad lighting, poor quality, poor composition, wrong color balance, etc.)

Typography- Create a headline called "Typography" in your headline font. Then, using your headline font in a smaller font size write: "Headline Font," then write the name of the font such as "Helvetica." Below that and in the headline font, write out the alphabet in upper and lower case along with the numbers and keyboard symbols. Follow the same process for your accent font and body copy font.

Vocabulary- Create a headline called "Vocabulary" in your headline font. Using your accent font, write out the words and phrases you want to use consistently in your messages. Do you have any images that reinforce your vocabulary? If so, place them next to your vocabulary words.

Logo Usage Guidelines- Create a headline called "Logo Usage Guidelines" in your headline font.

- Place each version of your logo on the page.
- Define when to use each logo. For example: "Use white logo on dark colored backgrounds or light photos. Use full-colored logo for digital screens. Use primary colored logo for vinyl decal vehicle wraps and stickers."

- Show examples of unauthorized logo usage. No squashing, stretching, or using unauthorized colors.
- Clear Space- Indicate the minimum amount of space surrounding your logo to prevent it from getting crowded by paragraphs, headlines, and other design elements that would make it difficult to read.

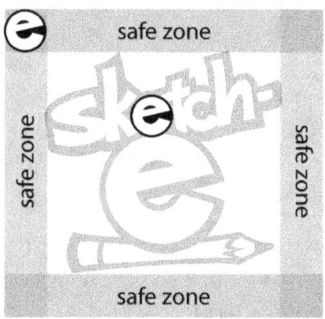

Tagline- Create a headline called "Tagline" in your headline font. Write out your tagline using your accent font and explain when it should be used. Most often this will appear next to your logo. Most tagline usage guidelines suggest that the tagline appear when the logo is seen for the first time, such as on the cover of a document but not on subsequent pages, the introduction to a video, or on a business card. Sometimes it can look weird on apparel such as hats and shirts so companies will put the tagline on a sleeve or the back of a baseball hat.

Examples- Design two or three marketing pieces that incorporate fonts, images, tagline, colors/textures, phrases. These could be packaging designs, a website page, catalog page, letterhead, business card, envelope design, etc.

Feel free to include pages for your business creed, mission statement, vision statement, values, and anything else that will help guide the decisions your company makes.

Evaluate each page to determine if a shape filled with a texture, color, or image can reinforce your message on each page. If so, add it and see how it looks.

Your **Brand Bible** is a visible manifestation of your brand. It affirms the personality of your company, who it serves, and how it serves them in the form of an easy-to-send-and-view document.

Use it to train your employees. Save a pdf of it to a file server like Google docs or your website, along with copies of your logos, brand images, patterns and textures, and fonts so you can easily share them with your employees and vendor partners, so they know what your brand is all about.

Congratulations!

You've got a logo, tagline, and a **Brand Bible** that secures your brand's look and feel. Your brand is on solid footing. You are armed to the teeth and prepared to battle for the hearts and minds of your customers. I'm so proud! <sniff> Now let's go put your brand into action and take over the world!

PART V
Putting Your Brand To Work

"The path to success is to take massive, determined action."

– Tony Robbins

Everything your company does or says should be steeped in your brand in order to increase its potency and integrity. In E- Establish Your Brand Adjectives I introduced a **brand matrix** that can help you evaluate whether or not an idea is more or less consistent with your brand. Another great metaphor you can use is a **brand lens**. A glass lens can filter out undesirable light rays and can magnify objects and bring them into focus. You can use your **Brand Bible** as a **brand lens** to filter out ideas that don't reinforce your brand and you can use it to identify ideas that focus and magnify your marketing and communication, building design, website design, uniforms, dress code, advertising, charities, sponsorships, and even your corporate events. Or, you can disregard it and suffer the consequences.

In Part V we will put all of these brand elements to work to design your print and digital marketing materials, design interiors and exteriors, select clothing and uniforms, define your business terminologies, name your products or businesses, produce your podcasts and videos, and develop your social media platforms.

Print and Digital Graphic Design

There are three responses to a piece of design – yes, no, and WOW! Wow is the one to aim for."

— *Milton Glaser - celebrated graphic designer*

You've got an amazing product or service, so you've got to spread the word! Whether your tools of choice to reach your customers are the digital variety like emails, websites, YouTube videos, and social media, or the printed variety like flyers, print ads, and brochures, each piece should share the same look and feel. When your customers see that your website appears to be cut from the same cloth as your podcast cover page, Facebook page, YouTube thumbnails, email ads, social media channels, printed flyers, and packaging, the impressions accumulate to create a powerful singular impression.

Use your fonts, colors, textures, images, voice, and vocabulary to compose the messages for your print and digital media. Use your creativity to filter themes like March Madness, Halloween, and Valentine's Day through your **brand lens**. Your audience should be able to quickly identify your company brand elements in EVERYTHING you design, even when it's themed.

Need help finding a designer? No worries! Online resources like fiverr.com, freelancer.com, and 99designs are plentiful. You can also search for design firms in your area if you prefer more traditional face-to-face communication.

Any designer worth his or her salt will have a portfolio, with samples of their work at the ready. Most have excellent websites that show off their creativity.

As you browse designer portfolios, look for pieces that have a similar look and feel to the brand you want to create for your company. It's true that many designers have creative versatility, but it's also true that they have a natural tendency to be exceptionally good in a specific design genre.

Designers coordinate their process with art directors, copy writers, and clients to develop the final piece. Good designers will give credit where credit is due. When interviewing a designer, ask questions about portfolio pieces that catch your eye. Find out what their process is like and how they make their creative decisions. Why did they use a certain font? Who wrote the copy and came up with the headline? What inspired their idea? What parts of the project were they responsible for? What direction did they receive from the art director? How long did it take? How many revisions? What would a design like that cost? Asking these kinds of questions helps you develop a comprehensive appreciation for their services.

Before you set your designer loose on creating marketing materials, share your brand bible and brand strategy with them. You can be assured that the ads and marketing materials your designer creates will be on-brand when you do.

Create an On-brand Space

Our environments and settings help convey specific feelings that motivate and inspire us. Environments like sandy beaches, blue skies, and palm trees help set the stage for relaxation, while movie theaters are designed by their very architecture to focus our full attention on the big screen. Regardless of the business you're in, you have two groups of people that benefit from an immersive brand experience. Your employees and customers. Your employees need to know and feel that the brand emanates from the heart of the business and isn't just window dressing for customers. Your customers or clients need to feel the personality and distinction of your brand, whether they walk into a real-world space or a virtual one.

Dress (Your Office Space) For Success

Whether your products are sold online or in a traditional retail store, one thing is certain, your employees work in the real world. They have desks, offices, cubicles, and work in warehouses. Some employees work remotely from home. Your corporate office, boardroom, reception area, and employee workspaces are incubators of brand ambassadors, so do everything you can to create a workspace that reinforces your brand's image and personality. The space you create informs the employees, vendors, partners, and everyone else that you are special, distinct, and purposeful in your message.

I once visited the Monster Beverage Corporation's headquarters in Corona, California. Their brand is strongly associated with irreverent motorsports, so I was pleasantly surprised to find that all of their concrete floors had been marred intentionally with motorcycle burnouts before the furniture was brought in. It gave the space a very authentic badass feel.

 *Take Action*

Paint your corporate walls with your brand colors, hang up images that you use in your marketing and advertising, mount your slogans on the walls. Print posters, create desktop patterns and screens savers, and give them to your employees who can enjoy them, even if they work remotely. Turn your space into your brand church so those who enter can be converted and then go out to spread your good news!

Retail Space

Your retail space should look and feel so distinct that your customers could be brought into your store blindfolded and be able recognize your business within a few seconds of having the blindfold removed. You should have your colors, textures, logos, surfaces and materials on your walls, shelving, displays, ceiling and floor. They should be designed to tastefully frame and feature your products or services, not distract from them. It is a plate upon which the steak is served. The plate shouldn't be more important than the steak.

Your space should also be designed for function. If you own a fast-food restaurant you don't want your colors, surfaces, textures to be warm soothing and relaxing. You want an environment that gets your customers up and moving so you can make room for the next ones.

Disney is unsurpassed at creating an immersive branded experience that provides an escape from real life. I recently visited Batuu in Disneyland's Galaxy's Edge and nearly cried for joy. Disney Imagineers filtered and magnified every sensory experience through the Star Wars brand lens to maintain a highly realistic otherworldly illusion. Stormtroopers in polished white armor guarded the plaza from the rooftops. The low walls that lined the walkways were intentionally crumbling and distressed to give the appearance that they and the city had been built hundreds of years ago. Maintenance employees emptied the trash wearing full Batuu costumes and Wookies wandered the roadways trying to strike up conversations in their native Shyriiwook tongue. (Lest you think me an overly zealous Star Wars fan I didn't know the name of the Wookie language off the top of my head and had to look it up!) You might think the bathrooms would be an acceptable reprieve from the Star Wars brand investment, but you'd be wrong. They too, are literally out of this world!!!

Disneyland is an extreme example but let their attention to detail inspire you.

 *Take Action*

Paint your walls using colors that match your brand colors. Use your brand pattern, textures, or image from your **Brand Bible** to wallpaper an accent wall or two. Build cabinets, countertops and wainscots using materials you selected in Part III. Select furniture that uses your brand's colors, patterns and textures. Design signs, nameplates, and office room placards using the fonts on your brand materials.

Write a description of your interior and exterior design in your workbook.

Wear Your Brand

"Style is a way to say who you are without having to speak."

– *Rachel Zoe- fashion designer.*

What we wear makes a lasting first impression that is difficult, if not impossible, to change.

I interviewed a director of photography for a television series I was producing, and this guy showed up riding an old-fashioned motorcycle, wearing dirty jeans, old shoes and one of those farmer-style baseball hats that had frayed threads on the bill. I wasn't impressed. His "packaging" informed me that he was creative and flexible, but I also assumed that he wasn't very successful or talented. Without being conscious of it I almost dismissed him from the start and would have, if I hadn't already scheduled an hour to visit with him. At the end of the hour, he persuaded me to give him a shot. I was apprehensive at first but, after our first project, I was blown away with his depth of experience, unique approach, and storytelling intelligence. The clothing he wore at our first meeting almost cost both of us a fantastic relationship. I wondered how many people may had overlooked him because of his packaging.

Whether you are a salesman, executive, or work on the front line, what you and your employees wear and how you look can influence customers' and clients' thoughts and strengthen your brand. Choosing your personal look is just as important as your business brand and requires just as much discipline. Your look should reflect your authentic values and personality. Don't be tempted to conform to what you think others expect you to look like or you risk eroding your brand integrity and confusing your audience.

A perfect example of this involves my friend James Lawrence, the Iron Cowboy, who gained no small amount of fame for accomplishing the audacious goal of completing 50 Ironman distance triathlons in 50 states in 50 days. The social media posts during his 50-50-50 depicted a lean, muscular athlete wearing a gnarly beard which became an iconic part of his brand image. When asked to speak to a group of executives at Nike he dressed to impress– shaving his beard and donning a button-up shirt and business suit. A Nike executive picked him up from the airport and had to ask who he was. When he answered, "James Lawrence, the Iron Cowboy, the executive said, "No you're not. Not looking like that! Nike is a brand company, so our first stop is the Nike outlet where I'll get you anything you need to look like the athlete you are." James hasn't shaved his beard since.

Clothing styles have inherent personalities, just like colors, fonts textures and images.

If your brand can be described as urban, relaxed, casual, and friendly, wearing casual sneakers, jeans, and a t-shirt would definitely reinforce your brand more than a designer button-up shirt and tie.

If your **brand attributes** are outdoors and rugged, it might be a good idea to swap your high heels and pencil skirts for trail-running shoes and cargo shorts.

If your brand is sophisticated, premium, expensive, refined, and polished, a trip to Hugo Boss, Armani, or Burberry would be in order.

To improve my recognizability and reinforce my clean, positive, high-energy brand, I shave my head and face clean, stay physically fit, and wear a perpetual smile. To draw an association with my brand development company, Ernburn, I wear comfortable black clothing with flame accents because I help "ignite" brands. After meeting me or seeing my photo, it's easy to pick me out of a crowd. If a business won't hire me because I don't look "professional" enough for them, what they are really saying is that they value conservative conformity over creativity. If that's the case, it's probably not a good fit for me either. I approach branding with the intent of breaking through traditional and conventional norms.

I'm not saying that you should wear dirty jeans and a worn-out t-shirt to an investor meeting because that clothing "expresses your individuality." That would be a huge mistake, unless you've become so successful that businesses come to you for money. When you get to that point, feel free to wear whatever you like. Until that time, I believe that, with some creativity, you can always be appropriately professional while still reinforcing your brand.

 *Take Action*

List your **brand attributes** on a whiteboard and brainstorm clothing styles and brands that reinforce your attributes.

Ask yourself these questions:
- What do you wear when you are most productive or most creative?
- Can you add colors or patterns to help draw a connection to the brand image you've created?
- If you are a sole proprietor, ask yourself, "What do I look great in?"

The answers to these questions will successfully guide the selection of clothing that will magnify and focus your brand.

In your *Ignite Your Brand* workbook, write a description of your look and how you dress that will strengthen your **brand personality**.

Employee Uniforms and Dress Codes

Dressing for success doesn't only apply to you as the leader. Uniforms and dress codes unite and inspire your employees, help customers identify them, and serve as advertisements for your brand.

When you walk into a Foot Locker, it's easy to spot the employees because their uniforms make them look like referees. It's easy to spot the differences between UPS and FedEx drivers based on their uniforms. When your uniform is a part of a remarkable customer experience, your customers will make a direct connection with your company. Without a uniform, that priceless connection can be lost.

Country Fair is a convenience store chain centered in, Erie Pennsylvania. Their name originated from their founder's appreciation of the hometown community feeling experienced in old-fashioned country fairs. They have a fantastic leadership team committed to their brand that is friendly, local, fresh, and family-centered. An obvious uniform choice for their front-line employees would be denim jeans and red gingham tops. That may seem over the top but consider uniforms worn by employees of Hot Dog on a Stick.

Hot Dog on a Stick calls their business an "American icon." That statement would suggest they desire a strong connection to Americana. In addition to their delicious corn dogs, they are famous for their fresh-pressed lemonade. Their uniforms reinforce their **brand attributes** and can't be missed.

According to Hot Dog on a Stick history, "original Hotdoggers wore polka dots but we changed to the famous and iconic outfit everyone knows and loves today. Our bright and eye-catching striped uniforms are 'Red, White and Blue with a Splash of Lemonade.'"

When I first started working at Maverik, their corporate dress code of slacks, dresses, and collared shirts must have been Xeroxed from the policy pages of Generic, Inc. How were Maverik employees expected to be inspired and use their creative genius to promote a brand centered on adventure when dressed wholly inappropriately?? I proposed a new dress code called "Adventure Professional" where employees could wear jeans, shorts, and anything clean and neat that you would expect to be worn by outdoor adventurers. This new dress code policy was received enthusiastically by die-hard brand advocates and was a sign that the executive leadership was serious about fostering an adventure-brand attitude. By wearing clothes that comply with the "Adventure Professional" dress code, Maverik employees reinforce the brand with vendors and customers who meet them.

What you and your employees wear not only affects how *they* think and feel, it affects how your customers think and feel about your business, so be deliberate about your uniforms and dress code.

Your appearance and the appearance of your employees should attract or interest your ideal customers.

"But what if my employees hate wearing clothing that inspires our brand?" When I've heard that question I respond with my own question, "Do you really want employees that aren't passionate enough about your company to wear clothing meant to inspire them and strengthen your brand?" If they aren't passionate, they're likely your biggest drain on brand enthusiasm. Cut 'em loose and let them find an organization that fits their own personal brand identity! You'll both be happier.

 *Take Action*

List your company **brand attributes** on a whiteboard and brainstorm clothing styles and brands that reinforce those attributes. Be sure to take into consideration working conditions, weather, temperature, and employee roles and responsibilities. If you run a retail business, it might be a good idea to designate managers or other onsite leaders with a different variation of your uniform, so they stand out.

Write a description of your employee dress code or uniform in your brand workbook.

Developing Names for Titles, Products, Services, and Companies

The beginning of wisdom is to call things by their proper name.

– **Confucius**

If you are building a strong **brand personality** that customers will notice, like, and prefer, you'll want everything you do to draw your customers' attention to it, including what you call your business, titles for your employees, and the names you call your products and services. The names you use can either strengthen or weaken your brand.

Employee Titles

Sales Associate, Manager, Customer Service, Marketing Department, CEO, and Technical Support are all titles that are both easy to understand and completely uninspiring. If you want to infuse the personality of your brand into your organization, try developing customized terminology that reinforces your brand values for position titles, meeting spaces, etc. It tells your employees and customers that your brand is more than skin deep. It's also a very notable point of differentiation and creates interest.

Online public fundraising platform GoFundMe was established to help people with great ideas find the financial resources to help them change the world. Two of GoFundMe's five core values are "spreading empathy" and "delighting customers." To reaffirm those values, the support department is called Customer Happiness. Those who work in the department are called Customer Happiness Agents. This title reminds employees that their prime directive is to truly understand their customers' needs and leave them smiling.

Apple's associates are called Geniuses because the company wants customers to know their employees have all the answers. The title is also a fantastic recruiting tool. Would you rather be an Apple Sales Associate tending a sales register or an Apple Genius working at the Genius Bar?

A few splashes of branded terminology can reinforce your brand's uniqueness, but a word of caution-- don't force it at the expense of creating confusion. Titles like "Value Creator" or "CONNECT Manager" may not draw an immediate connection to the person's role, nor hint toward a specific brand influence. So, don't feel like you need to force it. Use branded terminology like crushed red pepper. Just a pinch makes a big difference.

 *Take Action*

To create your own terminology, grab a whiteboard and list the vocabulary words you selected in Part III- Establishing Your Brands Look and Feel, then brainstorm additional terms associated with your **brand personality**. Next to that list, write down key job positions, shared office spaces/conference rooms and processes. Look for associations that make a quick and easy connection.

Write down some of your terminology in your brand workbook for future reference.

A strong product name will be easy to remember, easy to say, easy to spell and, when filtered through your brand lens, will create a quick mental and emotional connection with your company. It should also feel right and be different enough within your industry that you can trademark it and register a website domain for it.

Rob Meyerson, branding genius and podcast host of *How Brands are Built*, interviewed ten professional 'namers' (real job) and mentions two great ideas: Taking a break and purposely coming out with bad ideas. [8]

Take a Break

We all get brain cramps when we focus too long and too hard on something. Scott Milano, who is the managing director of a brand naming agency called Tanj, encourages people to take a mental break to kickstart the creative juices. "Even if it's a couple hours, or a day or so. Just do not think about it and try to come back to it with fresh eyes."

Try exercising, playing a video game, working on a different project, or staring at the drain in the shower. I get my best ideas there!

Take out the trash.

---

[8] https://www.businessinsider.com/professional-namer-brand-names-2018-8
Professional product namers (yep, real job), use a variety of techniques and strategies to come up with names.

Sometimes we stifle our creativity because we want to look good by only dreaming up great ideas. Try coming up with terrible ideas on purpose in order to break through the creative mental block. When you aren't worried about getting your ideas ridiculed in front of your peers or subordinates, you liberate your creative mind. I think that's how my team came up with Truck Norris– an over the top, Chuck Norris-themed truck for a Maverik sweepstakes prize.

Here are some additional approaches that I personally use, and I know others use, to devise great brand names.

Acronyms

Using acronyms is a great way to create memorable names for your brand. This is especially helpful for products with long names like the consumer version of the military's High Mobility Multipurpose Wheeled Vehicle or HMMWV. Saying HMMWV is a mouthful, so it was often pronounced "Humvee." Soldiers nicknamed it the Hummer and the name stuck when it was introduced into the consumer market.

Mars and Murrie chocolates are coated with colorful candy shells and fun to eat. However, calling them M&M's is shorter, easier (and more fun) to say, write, and remember! Acronyms also work well for company names. This comes in handy when the name of the founder, product, or service is hard to say and write, like BMW, a German automobile company known for precision engineering and luxury performance. BMW is a lot easier to pronounce and remember than Bayerische Motorenwerke. The same thing goes for assemble-it-yourself furniture giant IKEA, named after Ingvar Kamprad who grew up on a farm called Elmtaryd in Agunnaryd, Sweden. Can you imagine asking: "Would you like to go to Ingvar Kamprad Elmtaryd Agunnaryd for some meatballs, cinnamon rolls and bedroom furniture?" Thank goodness for acronyms!

Technology has advanced far beyond the telegraph, so when American Telephone and Telegraph dropped telegraph services in 1991, they changed their name to AT&T, Inc.

If your business name is long, hard to say or difficult to remember, consider using an acronym.

Creating an acronym is simple. Select the first letter in the words you're working with and try to create a word using those letters in the same order. Feel free to add a letter to make it a word that's easy to pronounce and remember, like in the Hummer example.

You'll know you've found a great one when it's catchy, easy to say, and easy to remember.

Wordfusion

Another effective naming process is something I call Wordfusion–creating a single word from more than one. It's the process of writing two or more words that describe your product or service and cutting them into pieces to see if you can create a new word that sounds like a real word while still conveying some meaning. Advertainment is a Wordfusion of advertising and entertainment.

My first product naming assignment at Maverik was for a large, scrumptious, chocolate chip cookie that featured coconut and macadamia nuts. The decadent recipe was perfectly in line with Maverik's over-the-top brand personality but calling it the *Chocolate Chip Cookie with Coconut and Macadamia Nuts* was too long and not sufficiently off the beaten path. Calling it the *Avalanche* was unique and in-line with the adventure brand, but it wasn't descriptive enough. In an effort to abbreviate the name we Wordfused the ingredients into a single word–*Macachocachicoconut*. When I presented the name to my VP he said, with some apprehension, "That's a mouthful." Exactly! I broke my own rules of "easy to say and easy to spell" in order to be memorable. Today, customers enjoy the challenge of saying *Macachocachicoconut* almost as much as they like eating them.

Bitcoin is a word fused from two product attributes, digital (bit) and currency (coin). The name easily defines the product. It's also easy to remember, easy to spell, and easy to say.

I can't omit a Wordfusion example of one of the greatest snack foods of all time, Cheetos! – A cheese flavored cornmeal-based snack from master snacksman and founder of Frito's, Charles Doolin. They Wordfused cheese and Fritos to create Chee-tos. God bless you Charles. It should also be easy to recognize that Tostitos! and Doritos are Frito's product brands because they use the same "tos" branding device to bring them into the same Frito brand family.

Letter Replacement

You can change the spelling of a word using letters from your company name to create your own uniquely branded name. This works exceptionally well in the English language because of the variety of letters and combinations of letters that make the same

Sounds		Real Words	Letter Replacements
ai	a(e)	gain, maim, stain	gane, mame, stane
ay,	ai	day, play, stay	dai, plai, stai
ea	ee	beach, read, speak	beech, reed, speek
ee	e	feet, peek, sheet	feat, peak, sheat
ie	ee	brief, chief, thief	breef, cheef, theef
ei	i, y	cried, pie, tied	cryd, py, tyd
oa	o(e)	oat, float, boat	ote, flote, bote
oe	ow	aloe, toe, woe	alow, tow, whow
ue	yoo	argue, rescue	argyoo, rescyoo
ui	oo	cruise, fruit, recruit	crooze, froot, recroot
kn	n	knight, knife, knot	nite, nife, not
ph	f	phone, phonics, phrase	fone, fonics, frase
ss	sc	bliss, chess, mess	blisc, chesc, mesc
wh	w	whale, what, why	wale, wat, wy
wr	r	wreck, wrist, writing	reck, rist, riting
ck	c, k	sick, lick, chick	sic, sik, lic, lik, chic, chik
se	z(e)	phrase, vase	fraz or fraze, vaz, vaze

sound. Check out this handy chart I made to assist you. If your business name has any of these consonants you can try replacing the letters in words with the consonant(s) from your business name.

Sheetz is a hip, exciting, fun, and quirky convenience store brand named after its founder Bob Sheetz. They are a highly successful company with over 600 locations in the Eastern United States. The incredible branding peeps at Sheetz have been using the "Sh" and "z" from their unique and interesting name to devise product names that draw a quick connection to the Sheetz brand. Names like *Shweetz* bakery, *Shmorez* donuts, Sheetz Bros *Coffeez*, are easy to recognize as Sheetz products.

When the Maverik marketing team was asked to create a package design for Maverik Candy and Snacks, the team suggested we brainstorm a name that sounded less generic. The name we landed on was *Trakker Snacks*. It was influenced by our penchant for unique word spellings. (Maverik is spelled without a c.) The word 'tracker' is a term associated with outdoor adventure. Both the word and the misspelling helped create a stronger association to the off-the-beaten-track personality of the Maverik brand. *Maverik Candy and Snacks* would have been a snoozefest!

If you have unique letters or sounds in your company name you can use them as letter replacements to create your own product names. It's also easier to find a website domain and get a trademark for product names with unique spellings.

Word Replacement

Another processes I use to develop product names is Word Replacement. It's the process of replacing words with others that are associated with your **brand personality**.

Maverik's Trakker Snacks had a variety of products including gummy bears, sour gummy worms, and peach rings. We could have easily used names for those products that everyone knew, but we decided to put in some extra effort as we felt it would be worth it. Taking branding to the next level is a part of Maverik's brand. We replaced "bear" with *grizzly* for our *Grizzly Gummies*. We changed the words "gummy worms" to *squirmers* for *Sour Squirmers*, and the word "rings" from peach rings was changed to *preservers*. Peach Rings became *Peach Preservers*. Each product name was an extension of the adventurous Maverik brand.

You can try the word replacement process by brainstorming variations of words that describe what your product or service does, what it looks like, and the benefit it provides. Then use a thesaurus to look for words with a similar meaning that alludes to the feeling or personality of your brand. You'll know you're on the right track when you find one that is easy to say, spell, remember, and which automatically feels like it belongs to your **brand family**.

Use an online naming service.

Companies like BrandNewName.com can crowdsource a name for you. Similar to logotournament.com and freelancer.com, you fill out a project brief to describe your brand and pay the nominal fee which includes a cash prize to the winning creative. Hundreds of creative people go to work and offer up their best ideas for your consideration. You browse and evaluate the hundreds of submissions and then pick a winner.

Think outside the industry.

Too frequently, competitive products and businesses in the same industry use the same vocabulary and terminology, which makes them hard to tell apart. Another fresh and interesting strategy to develop a name is to think outside your industry. This process requires you to get out of your head and stop thinking about your industry for a while. It's a great excuse to go on a walk-about.

One of my good friends helped establish an online book club service that helps businesses and groups center discussions on books. They followed their own naming process which included listing brand descriptors such as caring, empathetic, welcoming, friendly, passionate, knowledgeable, and uplifting. Terms associated with book clubs like read, gather, book, margins, shelf, bookmark, and book club would be obvious choices, but a member of their brand trust proposed names outside of the industry that focused on locations or settings that conveyed the *feelings* the team wanted their customers to associate with their brand. Instead of "BookClub" they settled on "Campfire" which reinforced the friendly, welcoming, caring, and uplifting feeling of their brand and stimulated tons of unique imagery and language to help them stand out.

Red Bull is the pioneer of the energy drink industry but was one of the last energy-drink companies to join the flavor innovation game. While Monster Energy and Rockstar were pumping out a variety of flavors, Red Bull was holding out. Its first foray into the field of flavor was based on color– The Red Edition, The Blue Edition, The Yellow Edition, and The Orange Edition. This was a refreshing departure from the names based on flavors that its competitors cooked up. It was also congruent with its brand name which included the color "Red." When it introduced its next line of flavors, you would expect it to follow the same color formula, but it zagged again, though this time it was on itself. Instead of expanding its flavor product line with names based on colors, it switched to names based on flavors like Peach, Coconut, and Pear. Its products would have been more in line with its brand had it stuck with its original color strategy. As a result, it has an incongruent mix of flavor names that weaken, rather than strengthen its brand.

Changing Business Names and Logos

As you go through the process of brand discovery and development, you may find your business name isn't congruent with the personality, products, or services you want your brand associated with. You might also find that your current logo doesn't reflect the image and personality of the direction you want your business to go. You'll need to make a change.

Changing your business name or logo is often costly and emotionally difficult. Businesses with brick-and-mortar locations have signs, uniforms and other items that are expensive to replace. Your company name or logo is likely to be well known and easily recognized by your best customers, so a change may be upsetting. Regardless of the financial or emotional challenge you face, making the right change at the right time can make or break you.

In 2010, AT&T, T-Mobile and Verizon announced a joint venture with plans to invest more than $100 million to develop a powerful mobile phone payment platform called "Isis." Millions of dollars were poured into product development and a brand awareness campaign, but a radical fundamentalist group of the same name began getting global attention for their heartless terrorist attacks across the globe. In order to disassociate itself from the ISIS terrorist group, the Isis technology company changed its name to Softcard. The story does have a happy-ish ending. A few months later, Google announced that it would acquire some of Softcards assets and intellectual property to integrate into its Google Wallet. The story underscores the powerful association people have with names.

Update Your Business Name

Naming your business is a two-part process. The first part is coming up with good options, the second part is finding out if any of the options are available for you to use.

Part 1- Come up with a name.

Use one of the processes introduced previously to help discover a new business name. It's going to be tattooed on your brain, your car, your website, and maybe even on your ankle, so make sure you LOVE it! It's a good idea to keep your alternate choices in your back pocket in case you find out your favorite choice is already trademarked or otherwise unavailable.

Part 2- See if it's taken.

Nearly every business has a website so, if the name you want for your business is already taken by another website, it's likely not available for you. If someone else has registered a domain name but you still think there's a chance you can register your preferred business name, you'll need to talk to your attorney who can look into it for you.

Before you consult with an attorney or accountant, check to see if your preferred name is available as a domain name by doing a name search on a service like godaddy.com or domain.com. If it's available, register the name right then. It'll only cost you a few bucks and if you end up not using it, you can think of it as brand insurance. If you own it, nobody else can use it to compete against you.

If the name *is* available, consult with an accountant who can recommend whether or not you should file your business as a DBA (doing business as) corporation, or an LLC. Each has different tax advantages and there are different laws for securing permission. (A

DBA is an informal business name that's not your legal business name which offers greater business name lattitude.)

If your accountant recommends you file for a DBA, you can do so with your local county clerk's office. They can tell you whether or not your preferred name is available and help you set it up.

If your accountant recommends you set up a corporation or LLC, you'll need to check with your state's Secretary of State to approve your business entity filing. You'll also need to hire an attorney or pay for an online legal service like legalzoom.com to conduct a trademark search then file for a trademark. This can cost a few hundred dollars or more, depending on which options you choose.

If your favorite name is not available, keep coming up with ideas using the suggested techniques I've mentioned until you find one that is available.

Logo Update

Time can fade paint, memories, and even logos. Many great brands update their logos to draw more attention to their brand, stay relevant to their customers, or adjust to evolving business objectives. Perhaps the personality or values of your company have evolved, and your business requires a new color palette, image, or type face that reflects that evolution. If you find your business traveling down a path that is no longer served by your existing logo, it's time to make a change.

When Maverik decided to leave the wild west in the dust and pursue an exciting, outdoor adventure brand, the name of their business stayed the same but its tagline (which was part of the logo) changed from Country Store to Adventure's First Stop. The Country Store logo had strong western design influence and would have been a detraction from its new brand direction. The business could not effectively move forward with its new brand without changing its logo.

The logo went through two revisions in ten years. Each iteration brought it in line with the **brand personality** the company intended to represent.

The colors changed from brown and orange to the new color palette of red and green. (Red for energy and passion and green for outdoor.) The product illustration was removed. The Country Store tagline was replaced with Adventure's First Stop and positioned above the logo, and the lower arch of the logo was flattened so the letters weren't so tall and skinny. This simplified the logo and bought it in line with the brands new color pallet.

After several years, the company realized that the subtle changes were not sufficient to distance the brand from the original western theme to the bolder, more contemporary, and aggressive **brand personality** that Maverik was becoming. The thick and thin anatomy of the letters were difficult to read on digital media such as websites, apps, and ads, so the logo was updated again to be bolder and easier to read.

third iteration

Maverik used the new logo immediately on its website, printed materials, advertising and on all new construction projects. It updated the signs on some of its busiest stores and developed a plan to update signage on other stores over the next three years based on a variety of criteria that, for reasons of confidentiality, I'm not free to disclose. Suffice it to say, they planned it out carefully because it doesn't make a lot of sense for the company to absorb a huge capital expense in the first year. Maverik also replaced any old signs that were damaged or worn out with new signs using the new logo. Within a few years, most locations represented the new look and feel of the Adventure's First Stop brand.

But you don't need to have a significant change in direction to warrant a logo change. Huge brands like Apple, Microsoft, Coca Cola, and Walmart, refresh their logos periodically. The good ones keep a design element consistent across each permutation.

Pepsi has metamorphosed its logo multiple times over the past century. Each iteration updated the typestyle while retaining the unique "wave" from the original logo. The wave is the smile-shaped arc connecting the P and C under the first logo. It has been one of the primary elements of design that unites all of its logos, that and the company's colors are the threads that keep the association of every logo rooted to the original.

If you believe your current logo is not serving you but you're holding off because the costs are intimidating, you need to realize that there is also a cost to keeping the wrong logo too. How long will it take to lose your customers to a competitor with a fresh, new, and exciting look?

If your new, healthy lifestyle means your pants now keep slipping off your leaner hips, doesn't it make sense to discard something that no longer serves its purpose for you and move on to something that fits? Buying a new pair of pants may be an additional expense, but they will enhance your new-looking (and better-looking) self, rather than your old, baggy pair that will do your new image no good whatsoever.

If you've made a bold decision to change your **brand strategy** for the better, your customers and employees will be hard pressed to know a change was made without a visible symbol of that change. Be decisive and move forward boldly. No one wants to follow the apprehensive or indecisive.

Branded Ads

Fortis Fortuna Juvat (Fortune Favors the Bold)

– Latin Proverb

In the 1990's, companies vying for a share of the personal computer market began running ads in an arms race of geeky technical one-upmanship, touting their computer processing and graphics display speeds as if all of their customers were fellow computer scientists who understood their techspeak.

Ads would feature an uninspiring photo of a computer parked next to a monitor and keyboard as if they were some kind of sculpture on display. A long column of technical specs would hang beneath a generic headline touting its faster central processing unit.

"Calculate complex spreadsheets faster with the brand new PowerMax 386/33 that comes standard with dual-level 128k backside cache, fully networkable, backward compatible, high-speed microchannel bus, with advance 256k RAM, 200MB EIDE hard drive, and a 16-bit graphics accelerator. You also get two USB ports, an 8-bit XT style expansion slot, two high-capacity 1.2MB floppy drives, and a port for most pointing devices."

Did they really think mom and dad knew what any of that stuff meant?

The biggest mistake companies make in advertising is focusing their ads on their products' exhaustive list of amazing features, hoping their customers will make the competitive comparison and arrive at the logical conclusion to buy their product as if each of the listed features tipped the scales in their favor.

Features and benefits *are* important, but unless you first get your prospects' attention, they won't be interested long enough to learn about them.

The basic strategy of advertising is all about exposing your message to as many of your targeted customers (reach) as often as you can (frequency). It's called reach and frequency in the advertising world and you pay out the nose for both.

Great brands are selective in their targeting, which means they don't spend money trying to reach people who are not likely to buy their products without a lot of persuasion. They also invest in producing ads that get attention and invoke an emotional response. This emotional response is frequently elicited through humor, empathy, or fear.

The primary message in your ads should feature the single-most important customer benefit presented in a way that grabs your customers' attention. Be brave and be bold. Use exaggerated visual or verbal metaphors to convey that benefit. After getting your customers' attention, quickly explain the features of your product that provide the benefit and include a link or URL to your website or YouTube channel where they can learn more.

Dos Equis' "most interesting man in the world" campaign doesn't even talk about its product. Dos Equis uses video footage of its brand ambassador doing interesting things with beautiful people. The benefit to the consumer is that they, too, will be perceived as interesting if they

drink Dos Equis beer. Its call to action is much more subtle than most, "When you drink beer, prefer Dos Equis."

 *Take Action*

STEP 1: Customer Benefit

Grab a whiteboard and decide on the primary customer benefit your product or service offers. Does the benefit increase social status, provide a unique experience, save them time or money? After you select your primary customer benefit, go deeper. Ask yourself, "Why would your customers want that benefit?" Is it because your customers want to spend more time with their family, enjoying their favorite activity, or something else?

STEP 2: Outrageous Metaphors

Once you've identified the customer's primary benefit, explore outrageous metaphors that make a visceral connection to the benefit. Write them on a whiteboard. If your benefit is increased ease, brainstorm ideas that are easy. Easy as… (fill in the blank) falling off a ladder, flipping a switch, Lego's, pancake mix, place and bake cookies. Come up with as many good and bad ideas as you can because brainstorming is more effective when you aren't eliminating ideas before they come out of your mouth.

With all of your ideas on the whiteboard, determine which, if any, can make a connection to your product or service. The objective is to get attention by making the benefit obvious.

In the following Old Spice ad, the customer benefit of the fragrance was that it made you smell like a man.

Old Spice was an old-fashioned cologne my dad used that continually lost market share to hip body fragrance brands until the "Smell Like a Man, Man" campaign debuted in 2010. It's over-the-top, all-your-wishes-will-come-true promises and creative video production process made it so remarkable and sharable that it generated 1.2 billion in earned media impressions and a 300% increase in traffic to its website. This means that if Old Spice had to pay for that amount of exposure on television, it would have cost Old Spice $1.2 billion. The results of this creative campaign helped Old Spice become the number-one brand of bodywash and deodorant in both sales and volume growth that year.

Carl's Jr.s' highly controversially provocative ad campaign that launched in 2005 successfully used sexy models to get attention for its extra-large burgers for men between the ages of 18-34. While most of the industry was zigging on healthy-for-you options and dollar-menu products, CEO Andrew Puzder zagged by featuring over-the-top thick burgers. The direction to be outrageous was based on the company's need to reverse a declining bottom line and compete with fast-food giants that spent five-to-ten-times more on advertising. When Carl's Jr. ads are getting aired at a rate that is a fraction of its competitors, it's imperative that the ads are noticeable and memorable.

"We need to be near the edge," said Puzder, "You need to remember our ads, so it's got to be close the edge and it's going to offend some people."

While being on the edge gets attention and drives business, it makes some people uncomfortable. The move away from that campaign to safer ground in 2017 has left advertising critics like David Griner yawning.

"Just a few years ago, fast food chain Carl's Jr. really wanted you to have sex with a hamburger. But now it feels like the brand barely even wants you to get to first base."

And it's not just the ad critics that share this sentiment. The controversial campaign was literally remarkable—it gave people something to talk about. Like it or not, the brand was relevant and on the lips of its customers and critics, earned more than $4.0 billion in earned media impressions and, according to Puzder, was a major contributing factor to its 5.5 percent same-store sales jump in 2005, and overall company turn-around.

So why does your ad need to be outrageous? Because you need to break through the noise of the world to get your prospects' attention. And unless you have your prospects' attention, you'll waste tons of money and time being conservative. As in the immortal words of Sir David Sterling, Founder of the British SAS, "Who dares, wins!"

But beware: Sometimes the pressures of rising competition can tempt you to focus your marketing and advertising messages exclusively on value. Those who give into this temptation invest their capital in feature enhancements, while reducing prices in order to create a competitive advantage. They end up with a brand that lacks emotion and with leaner profit margins. It's a no-win situation!

Charities and Sponsorships

Crime investigators use Edmond Locard's 'exchange principle' to help solve crimes. The basic principles state that when two objects are in contact with each other, they each leave a trace of themselves on the other. Fingers leave prints on guns while gun oil and gun powder residue leave traces on fingers. Shoes leave prints in mud which soils shoes. Clothing can leave traces of fabric in trunks of cars and fabric in trunk liners can get caught on clothes. The same principle applies with branding. When organizations work together or create an association, such as sponsorships or charitable donations, traces of each brand will rub off on the other. This is why great athletes want to be associated with Nike and Nike wants to be associated with great athletes.

Today, customers expect organizations to share their wealth. There are countless noble and worthwhile charities in the world, and businesses, perhaps like yours, are pulled in as many directions to decide which to support. With a little research, it's possible to identify charities that share your values and have a similar look and feel to your organization. Companies that make an effort to filter their charitable giving through their **brand lens** strengthen their brand by showing their customers their true values are in line with the ones listed on their websites.

Larger businesses are often targeted by charitable organizations and so they don't have to go searching for any to sponsor. Smaller businesses may need to go on a hunt for the right charity to sponsor. When you do find yourself evaluating a charitable organization, compare its brand bible to yours. Do your businesses share personality traits? Do you have a similar look and feel, values or audience? If you do, it's something that should be considered. If not, let it down gently and keep looking.

Tom's Shoes' brand was built on providing shoes to children that didn't have them. It makes sense that a shoe company would contribute to a shoe initiative. General Mills seeks to "champion global food safety, increase community food and nutrition security, invest in its hometown communities and improve global water stewardship." It makes sense that a food company is associating with a health and nutrition initiative. Disney's customer base are children and their families, so it makes sense that it would donate over 23 million books to children all around the world.

The same exchange principle applies to community and competitive event sponsorships. Each opportunity has its inherent brand and personality, and it's in your best interest to align with those that match yours.

While I was working for Maverik, the owners often made generous contributions to help our local communities and organizations. They liked making those contributions on behalf of Maverik and most were a really good fit. However, in one instance they committed a sizable donation to the Utah Symphony. They believed that making the donation on behalf of Maverik would attract the more sophisticated members of the community– a customer segment that Maverik usually/always neglected targeting in advertising and marketing messages. I explained that a transfer of personality takes place when an organization chooses to support another brand. A little bit of their brand will rub off on us while a little of ours will rub off on them. The independent-spirited, adventurous personality of the Maverik brand is in direct contrast to the sophisticated, metropolitan personality of the Symphony's. The sponsorship would likely result in brand confusion.

The request to sponsor the Symphony demonstrated a lack of connection to Maverik's target customer. Maverik had created an environment catered to a customer segment with opinions and preferences that are not shared by the majority of symphony enthusiasts. There are always exceptions to the rule, but the majority of symphony enthusiasts would rather not purchase food and beverages from convenience stores. They also drive expensive cars and prefer top-tier fuel with additives and detergents unavailable at Maverik stores.

My team and I felt the donation would do more harm than good and we recommended that the owners make the donation on behalf of one of their other companies, like their hotel or bank.

As your business grows, you'll receive lots of opportunities to share your wealth with worthy charities. Be generous and filter sponsorship opportunities through your brand lens. When you do, you'll increase your brand potency while staying focused on your most valuable customer segment(s).

Three, two, one, liftoff!

Whew! I've just unloaded nearly three decades of branding experience on you and you're still standing!

You understand that your brands start with a unique **brand spark** that describes what makes your business different and special. It is the inspiration for all of your advertising and marketing and the most important message you can convey. You know how to identify your target customer(s) and understand how important it is to focus on them with undeterred commitment. You have put into words the **core belief** that drives you so that others can share in your passion for why you provide the products and services you do. You know how to describe your brand to tailor the development of its unique look and feel through colors, patterns, textures, images, typography vocabulary and sound. You've even designed your own **Brand Bible** and know how to use it to influence the day-to-day marketing and advertising decisions you make in graphic design, branded space, clothing, terminology, naming, advertising, and charitable giving.

Wow! You know more about brand development than most seasoned marketing executives. I'm not kidding! Now go ignite a brand that gets attention, enthuses employees, makes money, and helps you make a difference in the world. Go build a brand that doesn't suck!

Afterword

Thank you for reading this book. It took me much longer to write than I ever thought it would and it was much more difficult than climbing Mount Kilimanjaro or finishing an Ironman. My shoulder devil tried to persuade me to give up several times with voices like, "Does the world really need another book on branding? Do you really think you're going to offer a new perspective? Does anyone really care?" Despite being tempted to pursue the path of least resistance, I told that little shoulder devil to go to heck!

I hope that you've been able to feel my love for brand development as you read this book. I believe underdeveloped brands are the basis for lackluster business performance and low employee morale. My superpower is the ability to recognize brand deficiencies and to ask the right questions that help you discover your **brand spark**. I have the creative production experience to help develop the appropriate visual and verbal brand language to connect with your core customers in a remarkable way.

I speak and consult on branding. I also offer an online branding course that walks you, step-by-step, through remarkable brand development. I'm the melding of a branding professor and personal trainer – clearly teaching the principles and concepts, then holding you accountable to stick with the program so you can achieve your desired results.

If any of these ideas spark your curiosity, point your browser to http://www.ernburn.com.

Thank you!

About the Author

After studying illustration at Utah State University, Ernie was recruited to be a concept and storyboard artist for Salt Lake City advertising agency, Dahlin Smith White. Two years later he established a creative production studio called 8fish that became well-known for animation, video production, ad design, writing, and brand development for a variety of clients including regional convenience store chain Maverik, Inc.. Ten years later he accepted an executive position at Maverik where he led a rebranding effort that transformed it from an old western brand into a $3 billion adventure brand. Ernie left Maverik in 2018 to consult and present on brand development because, well, he's really good at it.

Self diagnosed with Hyperactive Productivity Disorder, Ernie loves to draw, trail run, compete in triathlons, wake board, do yoga, lift weights, camp, mountain bike, watch movies, eat junk food and spend time with his family and 7 brothers. Ask him about his real life allergies to exercise and the TV travel show he hosted.